A LIFE'S WORK

Achieving full and fulfilling employment

edited by

Nick Burkitt

30-32 Southampton St
London WC2E 7RA
Tel: 020 7470 6100
Fax: 020 7470 6111
postmaster@ippr.org.uk
www.ippr.org
Registered charity 800065

The Institute for Public Policy Research is an independent charity whose purpose is to contribute to public understanding of social, economic and political questions through research, discussion and publication. It was established in 1988 by leading figures in the academic, business and trade-union communities to provide an alternative to the free market think tanks.

IPPR's research agenda reflects the challenges facing Britain and Europe. Current programmes cover the areas of economic and industrial policy, Europe, governmental reform, human rights, defence, social policy, the environment and media issues.

Besides its programme of research and publication, IPPR also provides a forum for political and trade union leaders, academic experts and those from business, finance, government and the media, to meet and discuss issues of common concern.

Production & design by **EMPHASIS**
ISBN 1 86030 163 0
© IPPR 2001

Contents

Acknowledgements

We are very grateful to the following organisations who generously supported the IPPR's Future of Work Project, of which this book is a part: the Chartered Institute of Personnel and Development, Deloitte and Touche Consulting, the Public and Commercial Services Union, and Siemens Business Services. Thanks also to Paul Thompson for help with running the project and for reading the proofs.

About the authors

Nick Burkitt is a Research Fellow at IPPR. He was previously a Senior Researcher at the Low Pay Unit, and a Research Executive at Millward Brown International.

David Coats is head of the Economic and Social Affairs Department of the Trades Union Congress

Mark Corney is Director of MC Consultancy

Laura Edwards manages IPPR's qualitative research projects. She was previously a Research Manager at Opinion Leader Research.

Mike Emmott is an adviser at the Chartered Institute of Personnel and Development

Richard Freeman is Co-director of the Centre for Economic Performance at the London School of Economics, and Ascherman Professor of Economics at Harvard

Francis Green is Professor of Economics at the University of Kent. He also acts as an occasional consultant to the DfEE, and has served on the Research Advisory Group in support of the National Skills Task Force.

David Guest is Professor of Organisational Psychology and Human Resource Management, at The Management Centre, King's College, London. He is a member of the editorial advisory board of a number of journals and a Council Member of the Tavistock Institute.

Lisa Harker is IPPR's Research Director, a trustee of Daycare Trust and author of various reports on work-life balance issues in different European countries.

Dominic Johnson is Head of Employee Relations at the Confederation of British Industry.

Suzan Lewis is Professor of Organisational and Work-Life Psychology at Manchester Metropolitan University, a director of the Work-Life Research Centre (W-LRC) and co-editor of the international journal Community, Work and Family.

Peter Robinson is Senior Economist at IPPR.

Adair Turner is currently Vice-Chairman of Merrill Lynch Europe and director of a number of media and internet companies. He is also a visiting professor at the London School of Economics. From 1995-99 he was Director-General of the Confederation of British Industry and before that a director of McKinsey & Company, the international firm of management.

Overview and recommendations
Nick Burkitt and Peter Robinson

Unemployment in 2001 was at its lowest level for a generation. Along with the introduction of a new set of employment rights, the labour market appeared to offer opportunity and security in a way that would have been unthinkable a decade ago. But the goal of 'full and fulfilling employment' in Britain is still some way off. Not only do some groups and some parts of the country suffer from unacceptably low levels of employment, the quality of many jobs still leaves much to be desired.

This book sets out an agenda for employment policy in the first decade of the 21st century. It looks at ways of bringing more people into paid jobs and improving the quality of working people's lives. It does so by looking at the evidence on what is happening in the world of work and at what the policy options will be for the British government over the coming years. The goal is to encourage informed debate and especially to encourage policy makers to look at the various aspects of employment policy together. We make recommendations on what the priority areas for government action should be and what policy levers it could use.

This chapter sets out the areas where there will be pressure for government action in the next few years. It also discusses the major trends in the labour market, which are discussed in detail in the following chapters. First, though, we set out our vision of what we would like to see in the labour market of 2010.

An ideal labour market in 2010

- *Full employment would have been restored – meaning an ILO unemployment rate of around four per cent, and over 80 per cent of working-age people in employment.*

The UK should be able to attain an ILO unemployment rate of 4 per cent by 2004. Normal cyclical variations of the kind seen in the immediate post-war period would see the rate fluctuate between just under 4 per cent and up to 5 per cent. The increase in the employment rate to 80 per cent by 2010 would be the minimum necessary to tackle high levels of economic inactivity amongst key target groups. The American experience in the late 1990s, described by Richard Freeman in Chapter 1, shows the power of sustained full employment to temper the rising wage and income inequality that has scarred the Anglo-Saxon countries, and to address other social ills that seemed insoluble, including crime and even teenage pregnancy. As Chapter 2 points out, a number of smaller European economies have also restored something close to full employment. The above targets match the ambitions of EU partners such as Sweden who have put full employment at the top of their agendas.

- *Employment rates would have risen for all excluded groups, including the over-50s, disabled people, lone parents and ethnic minorities, and in all parts of the country.*

Overall employment differentials would have narrowed on all dimensions. As discussed in Chapter 2, an extra three quarters of a million men over 50 would need to be in work to restore their employment rate to that of the late 1970s. Employment amongst ethnic minority groups would need to rise by 400,000 to match the white population. Halving the difference between the employment rates of the disabled and the overall population would mean an extra 900,000 in work. The elimination of child poverty would appear in the Government's own terms to involve a major increase in employment, especially among lone parents. If all parents who can work do so there would need to be an extra 1.5 million jobs. In addition all local labour markets would need to have employment rates above 70 per cent so as to make them more even across the country.

- *Intensive and personalised support offered by a well resourced and staffed Working Age Agency would have been key to reducing inactivity rates.*

As discussed in Chapter 11, the allocation of spending under the New Deal programmes would have been re-weighted towards those groups suffering from high levels of economic inactivity. People leaving benefits would also receive more help in securing progression after they take a job. There would be publicly funded services directed at helping people stay in work, and then move on to better paid and more rewarding work than typical 'entry level' jobs. However, difficult questions about the relative priority to be given to securing higher employment rates and to better progression will need to be addressed.

- *There would be appropriate choice and options for people to balance work and other responsibilities.*

A better work-life balance in 2010 will not necessarily mean everyone working fewer hours or less intensively. It should mean people having real choices over their pattern and intensity of work, with the ability to strike the right balance as their life outside work changes. As set out in Chapter 8, state intervention should be focused on supporting people as they move in and out of caring roles, with resources focused on people with dependants, including elderly or disabled people as well as children. Government would continue to help spread information to employers about the benefits of more imaginative and flexible working practices for *all* workers.

- *There would be greater opportunities for people to participate in and be consulted about decisions in their workplaces* – either directly as individuals and/or indirectly through unions or other representatives.

More employers would have recognised the benefits described in Chapters 6 and 7 for employee satisfaction and company performance of more sophisticated 'high commitment' people management practices. The idea that employees are stakeholders in the organisation they work for, and that as citizens they have a right to be informed about major decisions affecting them, would also have become more widely accepted, and be reflected in company law.

- *There would be widespread access to a range of lifelong learning opportunities* – both inside and outside the workplace.

This would have been achieved with a more equitable division of financial and time costs between employers, individuals and the state. Both the demand for and supply of skills and learning in the labour market would have increased. The problem of inequality in access to training highlighted in Chapter 9 would have been addressed by the state helping individuals to access appropriate learning opportunities.

- *There would be equality of opportunity in recruitment, promotion and conditions of work* – achieved by having effectively dealt with direct and indirect discrimination by race, gender, age, disability, sexual orientation, religion or any other unjustifiable criteria.

In the first few years of the century, the Government will have gone beyond the minimum requirements of implementing the EU Equal Treatment directive in 2003 and 2006. It will have been actively promoting good practice by employers in the area of equality and diversity, as well as enforcing rights against discrimination.

- *The gender pay gap would have been significantly reduced* to match the best performance in Europe.

The share of caring roles and paid work between men and women would also have become more equal.

- *For those in work, income after tax and benefits would be well clear of the poverty line*, thanks to a regularly uprated minimum wage and significant support through the provision of in-work benefits and tax credits.

For those not currently in the labour market and especially for those for whom paid work is not appropriate, income would be above the poverty line.

● *People at all levels of income would be building up adequate pension rights* through the optimal mix of state pay-as-you-go and private funded pension provision, so all could have choices on the manner and timing of their retirement, on an income above the poverty line.

This book addresses the first six of these targets. Work at the IPPR is addressing some of the others. A broad research programme on achieving equality includes new work on age equality in employment, and on achieving race equality in Whitehall and its agencies. There is also work on whether current pensions policy has got right the mix between state and private pension provision. The tackling of poverty through the tax and benefits system is an ongoing concern of the Institute. These goals can only be achieved through concerted action across government, but almost all of them would fall under the remit of any unified 'Department of Work' in Whitehall (McCarthy 1997).

Policy issues and pressure points

Globalisation, new technology and the 'End of Work'

In the 1990s, many commentators painted a picture of the future where 'globalisation' and new technology would destroy jobs in the West (Rojas, 2000). Competition from abroad would destroy well paid American and European jobs, to be replaced by insecure and lower paid service jobs. Politicians talked about how to accommodate these apparently inevitable trends. However, as Adair Turner describes in Chapter 3, much of this analysis was 'Globaloney'. The world economy is not a zero-sum game where some must win while others lose.

The US and a number of the smaller European countries entered the 21st Century with near full employment. As Richard Freeman argues, the beneficial effects of full employment seem to have outweighed the predicted negative impact on disadvantaged workers of 'skill biased technical change' and trade with less developed countries. In America in the late 1990s, the lowest paid workers saw significant increases in their real wages, so calling a halt to the remorseless rise in wage and income equality from the 1970s onwards. On the other hand inequality is still high, and has not actually been reduced noticeably.

The economic cycle has not been abolished, and employment levels will rise and fall in the future, but the new 'knowledge based' economy is not a threat to employment. We can be fairly sure that IT will destroy more jobs than it creates in the coming years, but we need not worry about this. New technology will automate away some jobs, but this means freeing people up to do other things. There will be more IT professionals in the coming years, but the big growth will be in 'high touch' rather than 'high tech' jobs – we will see more care workers, nurses, teachers, and people working in a swathe of 'leisure' occupations.

Some of these personal service jobs are not well paid, but poverty wages are not inevitable. Wage differentials between top and bottom earners depend on cultural norms relating to what is acceptable, as well as on government policy. Some people will inevitably command a modest return in the labour market. The question is how much redistribution is possible and desirable to compensate people for these market outcomes, using the minimum wage and especially the tax and benefits system. Some of these jobs can also be redesigned and made more skilled by employers, and many of them are in the public sector, so pay and conditions can be influenced directly.

Full employment and welfare to work

Full employment is now firmly back on the agenda in Britain. All three main political parties are committed to it, even though this would have been unthinkable just a few years ago. The exact meaning and implications of the government's goal of 'employment opportunity for all' are still vague though. Chapter 2 suggests a more precise definition and explores the implications of this for the activity rates of lone parents, ethnic minorities, disabled people and the over 50s. The employment rates of all of these groups are responsive to the economic cycle and the aggregate employment rate. Much of the fall in the employment rate for men over 50 looks increasingly like a specific historical event of the 1980s and early 1990s and is capable of being reversed.

Inevitably, as unemployment falls the people still left outside the labour market will be the ones facing the most acute barriers to work. However, the American experience in the late 1990s should teach us that even those with the greatest apparent problems in terms of their 'employability' can find work in a very tight labour market. More resources should be devoted to them and assistance adapted more to their varying needs, including help with job search, advice, support and counselling and training.

A big question facing the government will be whether or how much it extends the principle of compulsion in dealing with a range of benefit claimants. The New Deal for 18-24 year olds was compulsory from the start, but the schemes for lone parents and over 50s began on a voluntary basis. These issues are discussed in Chapter 11. Other major challenges in this area will be finding and recruiting the staff who can offer the necessary services to a range of different jobless people and employers as well as deciding how far to help people to secure further progression after they enter employment. The 'low pay/no pay' cycle has not gone away, and the state will have a key role in tackling it.

Although this book looks only at policy directed to individuals, government will have to recognise in tackling unemployment that there are demand side as well as supply side problems. Although it is true that many unemployed people are not far from areas with relatively tight labour markets, as Chapter 2 describes some parts of the country with the lowest employment levels are a long way from any booming job markets. Specific measures to raise labour demand in deprived parts of London would probably be misguided, since extra jobs would not necessarily go to people from the area, but they are likely to be a necessary part of the policy mix in areas like the North East and Wales. The key is to link up the work of the Working Age Agency more closely with local and regional regeneration initiatives.

Although getting existing UK residents into work is the priority, there will also be significant policy issues for government to address in the area of international labour migration. The goal of the Home Office is managing migration to maximise its economic and social contribution to the UK. At present, only 150,000 people a year are legally entering the UK to work, but there are likely to be pressures to increase this from skill shortages, multi-national firms wanting to transfer their staff from offices abroad and indeed vacancies in unskilled jobs.

Quality of work and work-life balance

Partly as a result of low unemployment, the quality of working life has been seen as a more important issue in recent years and this is likely to continue to be the case. There are many different aspects to the quality of work, discussed in Chapters 5, 6 and 7. A key distinction is between 'intrinsic' elements – such as the nature of the work itself and the amount of freedom or autonomy allowed in carrying it out – and 'extrinsic' elements such as pay, job security and opportunities for development. There is also the psychological dimension of job quality, based on the nature of relationships at work and people's desire for respect from colleagues and mangers and for fair treatment. These last elements are embodied in the idea of the 'psychological contract' described by David Guest and Mike Emmott.

It is important to remember that not all of these aspects of 'quality of work' are within the power of government to improve, even if many of them can be helped by enforcing minimum standards. The qualitative research described in Chapter 5 also suggests that employees do not look to the state to help them in a number of these areas.

The biggest debate on the quality of working life has been over Britain's alleged 'long hours culture' at work. This is seen to do damage to families and lives outside work and to have an impact on workers' mental and physical health and their ability to carry out their duties safely. It is often said that British people work the longest hours in Europe. In fact this is only true for male full-time workers. Britain has a wider spread of working hours than most other EU countries, with more people working very long or very short hours and fewer people working a standard 35-40 hour week.

It is also often said that average hours are rising and that people work harder than they used to, partly because jobs are more insecure. Francis Green in Chapter 4 shows that average hours have not increased, but rather our relatively dispersed pattern of working hours has widened further and there has been some polarisation across households, with hours of work growing amongst two-earner couples. There is also evidence of increased work intensity – employees feel they are working harder than they used to. There appears to be a link between the use of IT and the fact that jobs in Britain require employees to be not only more skilled but harder working – a phenomenon labelled 'effort-biased technological change'.

Arguably, the problem that should concern policy makers is not so much long hours per se, but lack of choice or control over working hours and patterns. Many people who work long hours are professionals and managers who do so by choice. On the other hand many have to work long hours to reach an acceptable weekly wage or because they cannot find a job with shorter hours. However, the state has a legitimate concern about very long hours where they impact on health and safety and on family relationships and the ability of people to care for dependants. In these ways long or inflexible hours can impose external social costs that will not be reflected in market prices, in much the same way as environmental costs. The difficult question is how to find a mechanism for changing companies' and individuals' behaviour, given the minimal impact of the existing Working Time Regulations.

There is evidence that in the last few years, average working hours might in fact have fallen. The 2001 Budget (HM Treasury, 2001), using Labour Force Survey data, describes an annual average rise in the total hours worked in Britain since 1997 of 0.7 per cent, compared to a 1.1 per cent a year growth in the number employed. The modestly rising share of part-time work accounts for only a small part in the reduced average hours. The Treasury asserts that in fact 'a fall in full-time average hours has been the main driver, and this is likely to have been a trend rather than cyclical effect'. The explanation given is that in times of economic uncertainty, firms tend to increase their demand for work with more overtime and temporary work, while stability encourages them to take on permanent workers and reduce overtime. In the late 1990s and 2000, overtime hours and involuntary part-time working have both declined, as has the proportion of temporary employees (down from 6.7 to 6 per cent since Spring 1997).

Discussions about 'family-friendly' employment at the end of the 1990s gave way to talk of 'work-life balance'- a more inclusive concept, which embraces all workers rather than just parents or carers. The DfEE's campaign of best practice stresses that it is about everyone finding their own appropriate balance (DfEE, 2000). The government has used a number of different rationales for intervening in this area, including improving business performance and 'competitiveness', safeguarding mothers' and children's welfare, and encouraging equal opportunities (see Chapter 8).

Unfortunately there are limitations to the business case for work-life balance policies, which tends to favour workers with the scarcest skills or in occupations that lend themselves more easily to flexible working practices. If government is to provide greater help to vulnerable groups – especially those with caring responsibilities for children and other dependants – it has to make a case for intervention based on social outcomes and the enforcement of minimum rights. An argument for better working conditions based mainly on the need to tackle recruitment and retention difficulties not only misses out some of the most vulnerable people, it also puts the drive for work-life balance at the mercy of the economic cycle. Concern about the social impact of paid employment should not be confined to times of economic boom.

There has also been debate about other aspects of the quality of work – especially access to training and the issues around the flows of information to workers and their opportunities to participate in and be consulted about decisions in the workplace.

In Chapter 9 Francis Green argues that there is no 'training gap' in the UK, in the sense that the evidence does not suggest that UK firms provide less training to adults relative to firms in comparable countries. There may be a significant problem with participation in and the outputs of the initial post-compulsory education and training system in the UK but this would not lead to advocacy of statutory interventions aimed at raising employers' adult training efforts. There is significant inequality in access to training, with better qualified adults working in more skilled occupations receiving a lot more training than the less well qualified working in less skilled occupations. However, this pattern is by no means unique to the UK and might reflect quite rational action on the part of employers. The onus would appear to be on the state to help individuals in less skilled jobs access education and training opportunities to help them move on in the labour market.

There is some evidence to suggest a link between training and business performance and this link may be stronger in the presence of certain human resource practices. However, this evidence does not in itself justify state intervention in the absence of a clear argument in favour of significant market failure. To the extent that information about any link is lacking there is a role for public policy. However, policy needs to focus on helping firms across their life cycle to develop better business plans, assess the implications of those plans for their personnel needs and only then think through the implications for training. This suggests an important role for the Small Business Service and for initiatives such as Investors in People. Mark Corney in Chapter 10 outlines an impressive list of other non-statutory interventions.

There is less clear evidence on whether the UK faces a 'representation gap', in the sense that the looser legal framework for information and consultation in the UK has led to less activity than in countries where such practices are legally mandated. In Chapter 7 Mike Emmott argues that there is no gap, though in response David Coats argues that there is, in the sense that surveys reveal the modest penetration of high commitment employment practices in UK workplaces. There is further disagreement over how far direct forms of employee involvement as practised in many UK firms are made more effective by indirect forms of involvement through the presence of unions and institutions such as works councils.

There is agreement that employee involvement may be linked to improved business outcomes and indeed to increased employee satisfaction. However, this in itself does not make the case for state intervention in the absence of a clear understanding of the market failures that might lead to a sub-optimal level of involvement. There may a case for efforts to promote more widely the benefits of certain employee involvement practices, perhaps involving an ACAS Code of Practice as suggested by Mike Emmot. However, as a further respondent Dominic Johnson points out, the European Directive on information and consultation appears to violate the principle of subsidiarity in that it is not clear why the EU needs to regulate employee participation in firms not employing workers across the boundaries of EU states.

There is a more general and contentious point to be made here. During the period of Conservative government the Trade Unions looked to Brussels for protection of employment rights and indeed as a result, the UK labour market in 1997 was in terms of individual rights in many ways more regulated than it had been in 1979. However, the 'high-tide' of a regulatory approach to employment and social policy may have been reached in the EU, with increasing emphasis placed on the 'open method of co-ordination' based on best practice and peer pressure (Vandenbroucke, 2001). The European Commission Directive on Information and Consultation may be the last major piece of employment regulation stemming from Brussels, though in the areas of equal opportunities and health and safety the role of EU regulation will remain important. The agenda for possible regulation in areas such as work-life balance and training will be addressed at the national level.

Rights and regulation

Labour's approach to employment policy has attempted to strike the right balance between regulating to ensure minimum standards while retaining an efficiently functioning and 'flexible' labour market. This has to be the right approach, though of course striking that balance is not easy. A number of new rights for workers were introduced in Britain in 1998-2000, including a minimum wage, rights to rest breaks and paid leave, parental leave and to join a union, and new rights for people with disabilities. Existing rights and entitlements, such as those relating to unfair dismissal and maternity leave, were also extended.

Inevitably employers have complained about the 'burden on business' brought about by extra regulation and 'red tape', while the union movement and voluntary sector groups have complained that the rights have not gone far enough to protect workers. However, as many of the chapters in this book show, attention has been shifting towards other ways of influencing the behaviour of employers and employees and changing cultures at work. Increasingly, parts of the policy debate have focussed on how to make better use of voluntary methods of improving workplace conditions. There have been codes of practice (for example on Age Diversity) and greater use of challenge funds, for example on partnership and work-life balance, as well as more dissemination of information and advice to employers on good employment practice.

This implies a significant role for the social partners as well as government itself. They can make sure that where regulations are introduced they have broad support and are workable, and they can promote more enlightened practices in individual workplaces. The Low Pay Commission has been a relatively successful example of partnership in producing workable and enforceable minimum standards. The Working Time Regulations, on the other hand, were criticised by all sides.

One issue that has not received enough attention so far is the implementation of existing rights. The main reason for introducing rights and minimum standards is that society wishes to protect people from the weakness of their position in the labour market, because the market outcomes that would occur in the absence of such rights would be socially unacceptable. By definition, people who need statutory protection will be in a weak bargaining position. This means that a system of enforcement based on individuals challenging their employer through the Tribunal System is likely to be of limited use.

Unions have a vital role in publicising and enforcing rights and in making collective agreements that go well beyond legal minimum standards. However, to reach the people unions cannot, we propose consideration of a new proactive enforcement agency (see Chapter 11). It would go into workplaces, after complaints have been registered or using risk assessment, checking that the law was being observed, directing employers to advice and support services to help them comply where it was not and then imposing penalties if they still do not. There are difficult questions about the appropriate nature of the links between support services like the Small Business Service and bodies enforcing compliance with legal minimum standards. These issues have already been faced for some time by the equality commissions, which it would complement in areas they do not cover at present. Nevertheless, it is clear there need to be both more carrots and more sticks than at present.

The most significant policy issue over the next Parliament will be to identify those areas that need stronger statutory minimum standards and those areas where improvements can be promoted through robust non-statutory interventions. To justify statutory intervention we need to demonstrate that there is a strong case in principle for intervention and that a form of statutory intervention can be found which will prove effective. However, in itself even this is not enough. The government in the next Parliament will face numerous pressures for increased statutory intervention across a range of policy areas related to individual employment rights. Any government will only have a finite amount of legislative space and even more importantly political capital with employers opposed to any further intervention. It will have to pick and choose carefully which areas to prioritise. It is important to remember though, that giving a

Areas of potential pressure for legislation/extension of regulations affecting individual employment rights	
Work-life balance	Paid parental leave, paternity leave and more generous maternity leave and pay Rights to work part-time or reduced/ flexible hours after childbirth Universal rights to flexibility of hours/shifts/term-time working etc.
Equal opportunities/ human rights	EU directives arising from Article 13 of Amsterdam Treaty will require legislation on discrimination on grounds of religion, age and sexual discrimination, and amendments on disability, gender and race by 2003 (Deadline in 2006 for age and disability) Protocol 12 to article 14 of European Convention on Human Rights would ensure non-discrimination in enjoyment of rights Draft EU Charter of Fundamental Rights includes workers rights, but would not be enforceable
Minimum Wage	Potential pressure for a higher rate and regular uprating after 2001 and 2002 increases
Corporate governance	Company law review may require directors to take into account the long and short term interests of all stakeholders – ie employees, customers, the community and not just shareholders.
Protection of transferring employees	Revisions to the Transfer of Undertakings (Protection of Employment) or TUPE regulations designed to protect employees who transfer, especially in the context of the extension of Public Private Partnerships
Working time	Certain workers (people in transport sector, junior doctors and some others) were exempted from Working Time Regulations when implementing the EU directive in 1998. These exemptions will come to an end in 2003 and 2004, and there could be a review of the regulations in 2003.
Training for people in work	Pressure for statutory provision to raise overall levels of workforce training and tackle inequalities in access to training. This could involve the use of training levies for employers or individual rights to time off work for study.
Employee participation/ consultation	EU Directive on Information and Consultation proposed by Commission in 1998 would cover UK companies with over 50 employees. Draft flexible over procedures, but would cover developments in the business, structure of and prospects for employment and decisions likely to produce 'substantial changes in work organisation'.

particular policy objective a high priority does not mean that it has to involve statutory intervention – it also depends on the appropriateness of different levers for change.

This list of pressure points includes a number of areas where government has no choice but to act in some way. Even if the era of regulation prompted by EU Directives may be about to come to a close there are or will be Directives affecting several key policy areas over the next few years. However, the government does have choices about how quickly or forcefully it enacts them and can implement them in more or less flexible ways.

What should be the priorities for the next ten years?

In too many areas of policy, such as training or 'work-life balance', there is not enough clarity on what we want to achieve or what the main problems are that need to be resolved. The goals of social justice, quality of working life, economic growth and individual business performance can pull in the same direction – this book offers some 'win-win solutions' where they do – but often they do not. Choices and trade-offs have to be made. That is what government is for. And policy makers have to recognise the limits of using the 'business case' or arguments related to the so-called 'productivity gap' when the more convincing rationale for intervention might be related to social goals like equal opportunities or the welfare of children and other dependants.

Achieving the ideal labour market and better quality of working life set out at the beginning of this chapter will require cultural change among employers and employees, as well as government action. It will involve many different methods of driving change, of which legislation is only one part. We believe these are the key policy priorities needed if 'full and fulfilling employment' is to be delivered in Britain.

Recommendations for government

- Extend and strengthen statutory rights in the area of work-life balance, prioritising the needs of dependants and open to men and women equally.

- Adopt a more pro-active approach to equality legislation. The government should seek to legislate by 2003/4 to make discrimination in employment on grounds of religion, age and sexual orientation unlawful and extend the Disability Discrimination Act. The opportunity should be taken to harmonise some provisions of equality legislation and the powers of the equality agencies.

- Raise the rate of the National Minimum Wage regularly, so that it at least keeps up with average earnings.

- Revise company law to give greater recognition to employees as stakeholders in the organisations they work for.

- Bring in the revised TUPE regulations, including provisions on pensions, by the end of 2001.

- Give more priority to people management and development issues in support and advice for employers, for example through the Small Business Service; these should be more closely linked to businesses' own goals and based on more robust evidence of the links with company performance.

- Devote greater attention and resources to fully enforcing existing employment rights, as well as any extension of them. One option worth considering would be setting up a new proactive enforcement agency or 'Fair Employment Commission', which would publicise and enforce individual employment rights at the level of the workplace, linked to enhanced help for employers to meet their obligations.

- Give the new Working Age Agency sufficient extra resources to tackle high rates of inactivity amongst the over 50s, lone parents, disabled people and ethnic minorities. This would be easier to achieve under a unified 'Department of Work' in Whitehall.

- In the medium term, provide significant publicly-funded support for jobseekers after they leave benefits for work to improve job retention and help progression on to better jobs – with the Working Age Agency working in conjunction with the Learning and Skills Council and its local arms and advice services like Connexions. This should involve organising all these agencies on the same geographical boundaries.

- Recognise that in parts of the country such as the North East or Wales more jobs are required, not just measures to improve 'employability'. A new or enhanced set of policy instruments will be needed to generate employment in those areas.

Challenges for trade unions

- Help to publicise and explain rights at work more widely. This would include considering a proactive enforcement agency to help those workers unions may not be able to reach.

- Work with the government and employers to identify those policies that might help develop workplace training and employee involvement, giving these issues high priority in bargaining strategies.

- Argue for more generous resources for initiatives such as the Union Learning Fund and Partnership Fund and make sure these are well utilised by all unions.

- Make efforts to improve the skills of their own staff and representatives, so that they can play a greater role in developing better HR practices in workplaces as part of negotiations. Individual unions have a role in building on the work of the TUC's Partnership Institute.

Challenges for employers

- Support moves to strengthen both government advice and support services and enforcement of compliance with existing employment regulation. This would include considering a proactive enforcement agency.

- Work with the government and unions to identify those policies that might help develop workplace training and employee involvement. Help demonstrate that policies based on the spreading of best practice really can have a demonstrable effect.

- Put people management closer to the heart of strategic decision making, rather than treating HR functions as peripheral to operational management.
    - Senior management in larger organisations, including the public and voluntary sectors and central government, have a particular responsibility to send the right signals to middle management and line mangers, showing that company policies and enlightened practices – on flexible working or parental leave for example – are taken seriously.
    - Small and medium employers have a responsibility to give more consideration to working practices and HR issues, and avail themselves of the advice and support offered by the public and private sector.

References

DfEE (2000) *Creating a Work-Life Balance. A good practice guide for employers* September

HM Treasury (2001) *Budget 2001 Investing in the Long Term: Building Opportunity and Prosperity for All* HC 279

McCarthy W (1997) *New Labour at Work* London: IPPR

Rojas M (2000) 'Prophesies of Doom: Fallacies About the End of Work' in *World Economics* 1.1, January- March 2000

Vandenbroucke F (2001) 'European Social Policy. Is co-operation a better route than regulation?' *New Economy* 8.1 Blackwell Publishers

1. The curative powers of full employment: the US experience

Richard Freeman

At the turn of the 21st century, the US economy had enjoyed its best economic performance in years. Gross domestic product per capita had grown substantially. Manufacturing productivity had improved, and American high-tech industries had regained world leadership that many had thought was going to Japan. The federal budget deficit turned into a huge surplus, courtesy of the late 1990s economic boom.

Most impressive of all, from Spring 1998 to early 2001 unemployment hovered around 4 per cent with no sign of rising inflation – belying the belief of orthodox economists that the US has a 'natural rate' of unemployment of 6 per cent or so. The ratio of employment to the 15-64 year old population reached 74 per cent in the US at the end of the 1990s, compared to 61 per cent in the EU.

As the American economy went from strength to strength, more and more analysts have came to view the US as having the right institutions and policies for success in the modern global and internet economy. But the US economy has its blemishes as well.

From a European perspective, the major area of failure for the American economy has been in the distribution of economic rewards. While the economy grew from the 1970s through the 1990s, the real earnings of less skilled and lower paid workers fell. During this period income inequality, always high in the US, rose to levels that put the US 'off the map' for a normal capitalist democracy. The country developed a seemingly permanent population of homeless men; hungry families who used food pantries for their meals; a population of alienated disadvantaged young men; disproportionately in the black community; high crime rates that led to mass incarceration, particularly of young black male high school dropouts; high rates of teen pregnancy; drug abuse; destruction of social mores in inner city neighbourhoods; increasing numbers of single parent families with little or no child support from the absent male.

Many analysts and policy-makers came to view the social problems of the American economy as insoluble, or at least beyond the reach of standard policy interventions and economic incentives. Critics of the US model of capitalism latched on to these blemishes as reasons to avoid going down the American road of economic development.

The full employment of the late 1990s gave a different picture of the ability of the US economy to ameliorate distributional and social problems. While the US still distributed a larger proportion of its economic bounty to the well-to-do than other advanced economies, full employment – genuine full employment with unemployment rates of 4-5 per cent – has much greater curative powers on economic and social ailments than most analysts and policy-makers expected before the late 1990s boom.

There are three ways to study the impact of full employment on the distribution of income and social problems facing a country.

The first way is to look at time series data that compare social and economic outcomes in the period of full employment with outcomes in previous periods. This is the most natural way to study what is intrinsically a time series problem. However it has two difficulties: if we look only at the 1990s economic boom, we risk attributing to full employment the effect of other factors that differentiated the nineties from earlier years – the growth of the internet, the influx of foreign capital, changes in welfare policies, in policing policy and even in moral uplift or the drug culture. On the other hand, if we examine evidence over a long time period, we are more likely to differentiate the effect of full employment from the effect of idiosyncratic period factors, but at the cost of averaging the unique effects of the 1990s boom with those of earlier booms. It was precisely the failure of the 1980s boom to 'trickle down' to ordinary Americans that differentiated that boom from earlier booms and disheartened many social analysts.

The second way to analyse the impact of full employment on economic and social outcomes is to compare areas of the country with full employment to areas with less than full employment during the boom period. This controls for the effects of the 1990s period that are common to all areas but risks interpreting area-specific factors for the effects of full employment. To deal with this, one can compare areas having greater improvements in employment with areas having lesser improvements, though even here there are potential problems in generalising to the nation as a whole.

The third way to perform the analysis is to examine the behaviour of employed and unemployed individuals. This can be done cross-sectionally, by comparing unemployed persons with employed persons, on the assumption that (all else being the same) the unemployed would behave like the employed if they had a job or longitudinally, by examining how behaviour changes when the employed lose their job or the unemployed obtain a job. By focusing on individuals, this method fails to take account of potential externalities among people – the effects of unemployment or employment in a community on the behaviour of all persons in the community – which may be especially large for the young.

Given the problems with all of these methods, it is necessary to combine time series, cross area, and individual data, and other relevant information – for instance about other explicit possible causes of change – to reach the best possible assessment of what full employment does to an economy. This is what I have done in my various analyses of the effect of the economic boom on the US economy (Freeman, 2001, Freeman and Rodgers, 2000, Freeman, 2000) and what other analysts have done as well.

The major findings of these studies about the effect of full employment on US economic and social outcomes are summarised below.

Economic outcomes

1. Full employment raised the earnings of less skilled workers

With a national unemployment rate around 4 per cent and unemployment around 2 to 3 per cent in many areas of the country, the US began to distribute the gains of economic success more broadly, as Table 1.1 documents. The real wages of low skill workers rose in the late 1990s. The usual weekly earnings of men aged 16-24 deflated by the consumer price index rose by nearly 8 per cent from 1994 to 1999, after having fallen steadily since 1980. The real pay of low wage workers categorised in various ways also increased in the late 1990s economic boom. The increases were most substantial in areas with rapidly declining or lowest rates of joblessness.

Table 1.1 Change in real wages of low paid workers, 1996-1999

Percentage change 1996-98, all workers

10th percentile	8.7%
20th percentile	6.0%

Percentage change 1996-98, 20th percentile workers, by geographical region

Northeast	4.0%
Midwest	4.8%
South	7.9%
West	4.7%

Percentage change 1996-99, workers in low pay industries

Retail trade	7.0%
Services	6.8%

Percentage change in median weekly earnings 1996-99, full-time workers in low pay occupations

Information clerks	7.2%
Food preparation and service	5.2%
Handlers, cleaners, labourers	3.3%

Source: Freeman, 2000

---

2. Full employment arrested the rise of inequality

The late 1990s gains in earnings for low wage workers did not noticeably reduce the overall level of earnings inequality. What the boom did was to arrest the rising trend in inequality, so the fruits of economic growth were more or less equally distributed among the working population. This is in sharp contrast to the 1980s, when growth and rising inequality went hand-in-hand, so that the benefits of growth did not reach a large proportion of the American work force.

That low wage and less skilled American workers enjoyed real wage gains commensurate with those of higher wage and more skilled American workers in the full employment 1990s suggests that the plethora of analyses that attributed their economic problems to free trade or skill-biased technical change are seriously misleading. Full employment trumps whatever adverse shifts in demand for less skilled labour that trade with less developed countries or technology have caused. The US does not need trade restrictions or a massive skill-upgrading program to improve the economic status of persons in the lower rungs of the income distribution. It needs full employment – genuine full employment with rates of joblessness of 4-5 per cent.

3. Full employment improved the employment and incomes of the disadvantaged

The economic boom increased the employment of substantial numbers of disadvantaged workers, particularly blacks. The employment-population rate for blacks improved relative to whites, as many black workers whom employers had previously shunned found jobs. Welfare reforms that seemed conservative madness succeeded in moving many single mothers from dependence into the work force and produced an unprecedented drop in welfare caseloads. To see how far full employment improved the labour market position of the disadvantaged in the US, Bill Rodgers and I examined the employment and earnings of young black men in metropolitan areas that had low rates of unemployment for extended periods and other metropolitan areas. We found that the employment rate and earnings of young less educated black men were noticeably higher in areas with tight labour markets than in other areas. A sizeable proportion of these young men moved out of the 'underclass' of unemployed or underemployed workers when their local labour market enjoyed 4 per cent or less unemployment.

Consistent with this, at the national level, the ratio of usual weekly median earnings of all black full-time male workers to white full-time male workers rose from 0.71 in 1996 to 0.76 in 1999, and the gap between the employment-population rate of blacks and whites narrowed among persons 16-19 and persons 20 and over. Despite these advances, however, black men were still less likely to have jobs and were paid less than white men even at the peak of the boom.

4. Full employment reduced poverty modestly

When I first looked at the rate of poverty in the 1990s boom, I expected to see a huge drop. In the US poverty is measured in absolute terms, as the percentage of persons or families below a given poverty line. Thus, with a reasonably stable distribution of income, poverty should fall when the economy grows. This was not the case during the 1980s, when income inequality rose. In the 1990s, poverty did fall, with the rate in 1999 dropping to the lowest level since 1979. But even so poverty remained on the order of 10-12 per cent even in the most booming parts of the country. Full employment may be able to reduce poverty to 8 per cent or so, but not much further. The reason is that in the US the majority of persons in poverty consist of persons who cannot even in the best of times make a reasonable level of income. About 20 per cent are retirees; about 20 per cent report some form of disability that prevents them from working; another 20 per cent are recent low skilled immigrants. A related reason for the sluggishness in the rate of poverty is that the average poverty gap in the US is $6,000, so that increases in wages or employment may make people better off without bringing them above the poverty line.

Social behaviour

Much to the surprise of criminologists, sociologists, and others who study social behaviour, the 1990s full employment boom was accompanied by marked improvements in a variety of dimensions. In some cases, we have good empirical evidence that full employment contributed to the improved behaviour; in other cases, while the logic is strong that full employment operated in the right direction, the relevant studies have either not yet been done, or have escaped my attention.

5. Full employment reduced the crime rate

Administrative data on crimes reported to police and survey based reports of victimisations by citizens show a huge drop in crime in the 1990s. In this decade, robbery and burglaries fell in the US to levels markedly below those in the UK. While the drop in crime in New York City has been widely publicised around the world (and attributed to particular policing policies), the drop is country-wide. It has been greatest in areas of the country with the best labour market conditions.

Analysts who study the link from the job market to crime rely largely on area data. The standard study contrasts changes in crime across local labour markets to changes in unemployment/changes in the wages of less educated workers in those areas. If Massachusetts has an exceptionally large drop in unemployment or increase in real wages for the less educated, then Massachusetts should also have an exceptionally large drop in crime. And this is precisely what the data show. Three econometric studies, covering somewhat different time periods and area groupings, have found that crime rises relatively in areas with loose labour markets and drops most sharply in local areas with the tightest labour markets (Gould, Weinberg and Mustard, 1998; Raphael and Winter-Ebmer, 2000; Freeman and Rodgers, 1999). Based on these findings, I estimate that about one-third of the 1990s drop in crime in the US is attributable to the booming job market (Freeman, 2000). The decline in crime means a reduced supply of young less educated men to the criminal underclass.

6. Full employment reduced the welfare rolls

Although expenditures on single mothers and their children is not a major item in US federal or state government budgets, the growth of welfare caseloads and its seeming insensitivity to the business cycle led President Clinton to promise to 'end welfare as we know it'. In 1996 he signed Republican sponsored legislation that changed the goal of national welfare policy from providing a safety net living standard for single mothers and their children to getting single mothers to work and achieve self-sufficiency in the job market. Clinton's major advisors on welfare policy viewed the adoption of such draconian policies as a dangerous surrender to the Republican right. The reduction in benefits went far beyond anything that President Reagan had ever suggested in his efforts to curb US welfare spending.

Without the late 1990s boom, the new welfare policies might have been a disaster. But in the strong labour market, they succeeded beyond anyone's expectations. The booming job market combined with the new 'get off the rolls and get a job' policies to reduce the welfare population and to increase the employment of former welfare recipients. In June 1999 6.9 million persons received welfare, which contrast with 14.4 million persons receiving welfare in 1993. The proportion of the US population on welfare more than halved – from 5.5 per cent to 2.5 per cent. In a careful econometric analysis, the Council of Economic Advisers attributed part of this striking drop to full employment, part to the new welfare law, and part to the fact that the law operated in a full employment economy (an interaction effect).

7. Full employment has not affected homelessness or hunger

Sparse data suggests that the booming market has not noticeably reduced the extreme forms of poverty – homelessness and hunger – that grew in the wake of the recession of the 1980s. A 1997 National Coalition for the Homeless review of research conducted in 11 communities and four states found that shelter capacity more than doubled in nine communities and three states during the preceding decade, indicating greater demands on shelters at least through 1997. In its 1998 report, the National Committee of Mayors also indicated that homelessness had not fallen in urban areas. Since these groups base their reading largely on use of shelters, they could be confusing shelter usage with increased homelessness, but the basic economics of homelessness suggests that they cannot be that wrong. One contributing factor to homelessness is the price of rental housing, which has risen in the boom. Another factor is that a sizeable proportion of the homeless population have serious problems – mental illness, physical ailments, drug or alcohol addiction, or a history of crime – which reduces their employability, so that an economic boom is likely to help them less than other citizens.

As for hunger, the US Department of Agriculture's study of food insecurity in the US, based on a special supplement to the Current Population Survey, found problems that no advanced country can tolerate. The government defines food insecurity as lacking access to food to meet basic needs, but which need not produce outright hunger. Outright hunger is more severe. The 1998 study found that 36 million people, over a third of them children, lived in households that were food insecure. This is over 10 per cent of American households! About 10 million persons lived in households suffering outright hunger in 1998. The incidence of food insecurity was higher than average among households with children, especially those led by single women, minorities and households with poverty level income. Comparing the data over time, there appears to be no change in the overall prevalence of food insecurity in the United States between 1995 and 1998. Additional evidence of the extent of hunger in the US is the fact that emergency food shelters provided food to over 25 million people in 1998 – with again no evidence of declines in usage over time.

8. Full employment may have reduced the teen pregnancy rate

The other important change in social behaviour is that the birth rate for teenage women fell sharply, due in large part to a drop in the teen pregnancy rate. In 1991 the birth rate for women aged 15-19 was 62.1 per 1,000. In 1998, the rate was 51.1. Among blacks the teen birth rate fell from 116 per 1,000 to 85 per 1,000. Officials at the National Center for Health Statistics reported that for girls aged 15-17 the birth rate had reached its lowest level since 1969 (NY Times, 1999). These drops occurred despite a decline in the abortion rate among teens, which implies that the main cause was a drop in the teen pregnancy rate. The extent to which the booming job market has contributed to this development has not yet been ascertained, but economic logic suggests that it has played at least some role.

Conclusion

The bottom line lessons from the full employment boom of the late 1990s are set out in the box below. The most important message is that the boom improved the economic well-being and social behaviour of the disadvantaged. With unemployment on the order of 4-5 per cent for an extended period, virtually every measure shows that disadvantaged persons and those in the lower parts of the income distribution made significant gains: the earnings of low wage workers rose; inner city blacks got jobs; the rate of crime fell; teenage births fell; the welfare case load dropped; poverty rates fell.

Factors other than the booming economy undoubtedly played some role in these changes in economic well-being and behaviour. Criminal justice policies, welfare policies, increases in the minimum wage and in the Earned Income Tax

Credit, all contributed to reducing the problems that at the outset of the 1990s seemed incurable.

However at the heart of the US attack on economic disadvantage and underclass behaviour was the economic boom. Full employment proved to be a superb policy for alleviating the problems of the disadvantaged. It raised the well-being of disadvantaged Americans and altered their behaviour, by giving them the 'right' incentives and opportunities. It turned a huge budget deficit into a surplus. It may be trickle-down economics, but it's a lot better than the economics of apartheid, where the rich get richer while no one else benefits much, if at all, from a growing economy. It dominated supposedly adverse effects of growing trade with less developed countries and skill biased technological change.

But full employment is not a cure-all. There remain major problems of income inequality in the US. A sizeable proportion of the population – around 10 per cent – are greatly disadvantaged even in a full employment economy. Full employment is arguably necessary to resolve the problems faced by these persons and to generate the budget surpluses that can be used to help them and to deal with other social problems. Full employment is not sufficient to resolve all of these problems. Given the choice between some government program and full employment, the evidence says, take the latter. However the US can do even better if it allocates some of its full employment budget surplus to reducing the residual blemishes of social exclusion and inequality.

The message

1. *The incurable problems of the 1980s and 1990s are largely curable*
   - Full employment is more powerful than skill-biased technological change and globalisation
   - The behaviour of disadvantaged people responds to incentives

2. *Full employment alleviates the problems of most disadvantaged*
   - Full employment works better than most government programmes

3. *But full employment is not a cure-all*
   - Income inequality remains
   - Residual proportion of the population – around 10 per cent – remain greatly disadvantaged

4. *A full employment budget surplus can be used to reduce further the distributional blemish on US capitalism*

References

Council of Economic Advisers (1999) *Technical Report: The Effects of Welfare Policy and the Economic Expansion on Welfare Caseloads: An Update* 3 August

Center on Hunger, Tufts University www.tufts.edu/nutrition/centeronhunger/hunger.html

CNN (2000) 'US News Census Bureau: US poverty rate lowest in 20 years' cnn.com 26 September

Food Research and Action Center (FRAC) www.frac.org/html/all_about_frac/about_index.html

Freeman R (2000a) 'Does the Booming Economy Help Explain the Fall in Crime?' National Institute of Justice 23 February 23

Freeman R (2000b) 'The Rising Tide Lifts ...' ? Conference on Understanding Poverty in America: Progress and Problems (Sheldon Danziger) Madison, Wisconsin 26 September 26

Freeman R and Rodgers W (2000) 'Area Economic Conditions and the Labor Market Outcomes of Young Men in the 1990s Expansion' in Cherry R and Rodgers WM (eds) *Prosperity for All? The Economic Boom and African Americans* Russell Sage Foundation, NY

Gould E, Weinberg B and Mustard D (1998) 'Crime Rates and Local Labor Market Opportunities in the United States, 1979-1995' NBER Summer Workshop, 6 July 6

Langan P and Farrington D (1998) 'Crime and Justice in the United States and in England and Wales, 1981-96' *Bureau of Justice Statistics* October, Washington DC

New York Times (1999) 'Teen-Age Birth Rate in US Falls Again' 27 October

Nord M, Jamison K and Bickel G (1999) *Prevalence of Food Insecurity and Hunger, by State, 1996-1998* Food and Rural Economics Division, US Department of Agriculture, Food Assistance and Nutrition Paper Report 2

Raphael S and Winter-Ebmer R (2000) *Identifying the Effect of Unemployment on Crime* UCLA mimeo, January

Rector R, Johnson K, and Youssef S (1999) 'The Extent of Material Hardship and Poverty in the United States' *Review of Social Economy* LVII.3 September 351-387

US Bureau of the Census (2000) *Poverty in the United States, Current Population Reports* Series P-60-210 September

US Department of Health and Human Services Administration, US Welfare Caseloads Information www.acf.dhhs.gov/news/tables.htm

2. The challenge of full employment

Peter Robinson and Nick Burkitt

> Employment opportunity for all is the modern definition of full employment. The Government's ambition is that by the end of the decade there will be a higher percentage of people in employment than ever before. (2000 Spending Review, HM Treasury)

Full employment is back on the agenda of all the main political parties. It is not only an aspiration of the current Labour Chancellor. Michael Portillo has succeeded in getting the Conservative Party to commit itself to full employment and the Liberal Democrats have also committed themselves.

This would have unthinkable only a few years ago. Predictions of the 'end of work' were rife and politicians' ambitions were tempered by the experience of mass unemployment in the 1980s. Indeed the main reason why full employment is back on the agenda is simply that unemployment has fallen far enough in the 1990s, without renewed inflation, to put the UK within striking distance of full employment.

At the same time a number of countries, most importantly the United States, had by the end of the 1990s already succeeded in restoring something close to full employment, with a set of very important consequences, some of which were described by Richard Freeman in the previous chapter. A number of smaller European economies also provided benchmarks for the UK to aim at, with unemployment rates in a band of 3-5 per cent compared to 4 per cent in the US, and employment rates significantly higher than in the UK at the end of the 1990s (Table 2.1).

Of course politicians are not always quick to attach precise definitions to concepts such as full employment, with clear measures of whether or not it has been achieved. That is one of the main goals of this chapter. It also tries to explore the implications of achieving full employment for the economic activity rates of groups that at the beginning of the decade had very high rates of non-employment and it explores the link with another key government objective, that of eliminating child poverty.

Table 2.1 Employment and unemployment rates in the OECD economies, 1999

	% of the population aged 15-64 in work, 1999	standardised unemployment rate (% of total labour force) 1999	% of men aged 55-64 in work, 1999
Switzerland	79.7	3.5	78.9
Norway	78.0	3.3	73.6
Denmark	76.5	5.2	59.9
United States	73.9	4.2	66.1
Sweden	72.9	7.2	67.1
United Kingdom	71.7	6.1	59.4
Netherlands	70.9	3.3	48.8
Canada	70.1	7.6	56.9
New Zealand	69.5	6.8	67.7
Japan	68.9	4.7	79.5
Austria	68.2	3.7	41.6
Australia	68.2	7.2	57.0
Portugal	67.3	4.5	62.1
Finland	66.0	10.3	40.1
Germany	64.9	8.7	48.0
Ireland	62.5	5.8	61.7
France	59.8	11.3	38.9
Belgium	58.9	9.0	35.1
Spain	53.8	15.9	52.4
Italy	52.5	11.4	40.8
OECD average (unweighted)	**67.7**	**6.8**	**60.8**

Source: OECD Employment Outlook 2000

Government targets

The Labour government has believed strongly in setting itself more or less precise measures of key policy outcomes in the form of Public Service Agreement (PSA) targets (HM Treasury 2000). The ones relevant to employment as set out in 2000 are outlined below. They are the joint responsibility of the Department for Education and Employment (DfEE), HM Treasury and the Department of Social Security (DSS).

The way these targets are set out (see Box 2.1), with one set of twin targets worded in terms of increasing the efficiency of the labour market, and one set of twin targets worded in terms of tackling poverty, shows the status of employment at the centre of both economic and social policy.

Box 2.1 Key PSA targets for achieving employment opportunity for all

Objective I: to increase the effective labour supply by moving as many additional unemployed people and inactive welfare recipients as possible into jobs and active competition for jobs, and hence reduce structural unemployment and inactivity rates amongst those of working age:
- Increase employment over the economic cycle.
- A continued reduction in the number of unemployed people over the age of 18 over the three years to 2004, taking account of the economic cycle

Objective II: to counter poverty and social exclusion by helping welfare recipients facing the most severe disadvantages to compete effectively for jobs, adjust more quickly to economic change and so raise their incomes and life chances:
- A reduction in the number of children in workless households over the three years to 2004
- Over the three years to 2004, increase the employment rates of disadvantaged areas and groups, taking into account the economic cycle – people with disabilities, lone parents, ethnic minorities and the over-50s, the 30 local authority districts with the poorest initial labour market position – and reduce the difference between their employment rates and the overall rate.

The green paper *Towards full employment in a modern society* published in March 2001 (DfEE, 2001), did not attempt to define full employment, but restated a number of related objectives. The two directly related to employment were, over the next ten years, 'a higher percentage of people in employment than ever before' and 'raising the proportion of lone parents in work to 70 per cent'.

Benchmarking full employment

It should be straightforward to set measurable benchmarks for full employment in the British labour market. In the golden age before the 1973 oil shock, a claimant unemployment rate of about 2 per cent was taken to represent full employment.

The claimant count has been somewhat discredited as a measure of the level of unemployment. However, the relationship between the claimant unemployment rate and the Government's favoured measure of unemployment – the internationally agreed International Labour Office (ILO) measure drawn from the Labour Force Survey (LFS) – has been very consistent over time (Figure 2.1).

In particular the two measures of unemployment always follow the same trend over time – whenever the claimant rate is falling or rising so is the ILO rate. The latter is always higher, including as it does active jobseekers that are not benefit claimants. The two series tend to converge at peaks in unemployment and diverge when the economy is recovering. This is a result of the 'added worker/discouraged worker' effect. When the economy is relatively strong some previously inactive people are drawn back into actively searching for work and are added to the ILO count, which therefore falls more slowly than the claimant count. When the economy is in

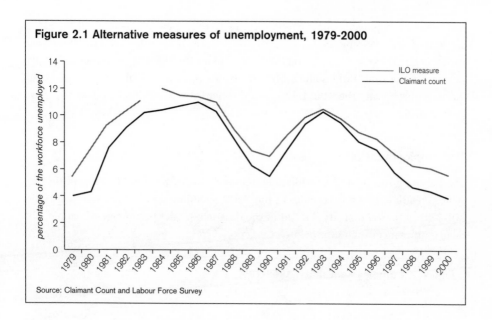

Figure 2.1 Alternative measures of unemployment, 1979-2000

Source: Claimant Count and Labour Force Survey

recession some jobless people cease actively to search for work and are no longer counted as ILO unemployed.

We do not have estimates of the ILO unemployment rate during the post-war golden age. However, in Spring 1979 the ILO rate was estimated at 5.3 per cent when the claimant unemployment rate was 4 per cent. In Autumn 2000, the ILO rate was once again 5.3 per cent when the claimant rate was 3.6 per cent. A claimant unemployment rate of around 2 per cent might equate to an ILO rate of around four per cent. This is also the rate now commonly referred to in the United States as representing full employment, though some of the smaller European economies have rates a little below this.

Some argue that traditional conceptions of full employment are no longer relevant in a labour market that has changed so radically since 1973. It is argued that full employment, as traditionally defined, was a commitment to male, full-time employment. In 1973/4, when the UK last had full employment, the female share of the total employed workforce was already about 37 per cent. By 2000 the female share was about 45 per cent and had been relatively stable since 1993. About 17 per cent of the workforce was already working part-time in 1973/74, against 25 per cent in 2000. Moreover, during the golden age of full employment the UK labour market was experiencing significant change in terms of the industrial and occupational structure of employment, and the pace of change in the 1990s was not any greater.

Setting a hard target of an ILO unemployment rate of 4 per cent would of course be far more ambitious than the current aspiration of 'A continued reduction in the number of unemployed people over the age of 18 over the three years to 2004, taking account of the economic cycle'. However, it is worth noting that over the three year period from Spring 1997 to Spring 2000 the ILO unemployment rate fell from 7.2 per cent to 5.6 per cent. If the same fairly modest rate of decline could be sustained over the next three years then the ILO unemployment rate would fall to 4 per cent by Spring 2003.

The employment rate

The Labour government's considerable caution is further illustrated by one of the five targets headlined by the Treasury in the 2000 Spending review (and restated in the 2001 green paper) that 'By the end of the decade a higher percentage of people will be in employment than ever before'.

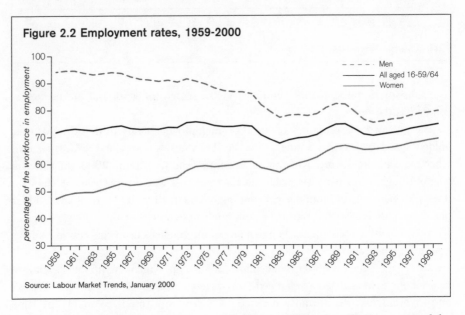

Figure 2.2 Employment rates, 1959-2000

Source: Labour Market Trends, January 2000

The post-war peak in employment took place in 1974 when 75.7 per cent of the working age population was in work. In Autumn 2000 the employment rate was 74.5 per cent. It would only take another 450,000 or so more people in employment to match this post war peak. At the rate of change in employment witnessed in 2000 that would be easily achievable within two years.

Of course the gender balance in terms of employment rates has changed significantly over this period. In 1974 nine out of ten men of working age were in employment and six out of ten women. By 2000 about eight out of ten men and seven out of ten women were in work. However, since 1993 employment rates have risen fairly evenly for both men and women (Figure 2.2). Male employment rates ratchet down during periods of serious recession, so if these can be avoided male employment should continue to recover. Meanwhile the post-war trend of a steady increase in female labour force participation seems to have slowed markedly. In the absence of further serious shocks we could expect employment rates to rise quite evenly across the genders, though exactly how employment rates evolve will depend partly on what happens to those groups currently with high levels of joblessness, as one target group – lone parents – is overwhelmingly female.

Alternate measures of worklessness

Workless households

In the 1990s there was a surge of interest in analysing the distribution of work across households, with fears that labour market and household changes were resulting in a polarisation of work between two-earner households and no-earner households (Gregg, Hansen and Wadsworth, 1999). There had been a significant rise in the proportion of all households where no one was in work associated with the early 1980s recession. In 1990 about 14 per cent of all working-age households had no one in work. This rose to around 19 per cent by the mid-1990s before falling back to 16 per cent in 2000. However, with ILO unemployment in 2000 below the rate in 1990, the headline workless household data appeared to show a worrying upward trend (Table 2.2).

The single most common type of workless household, accounting in 2000 for

---

Table 2.2 Workless households in the UK, 1990-2000

	Workless households		Children in workless households	
	Number (000s)	As % of all households	Number (000s)	As % of all children
1990	2,409	14.1	1,613	13.9
1992	3,043	17.3	2,219	18.8
1993	3,283	18.4	2,288	19.2
1994	3,391	18.7	2,398	20.0
1995	3,446	18.7	2,399	19.4
1996	3,444	18.9	2,344	19.4
1997	3,271	17.9	2,163	17.9
1998	3,237	17.5	2,156	17.9
1999	3,156	17.0	2,087	17.3
2000	3,066	16.4	1,907	15.8

Source: Labour Market Trends, January 2001- LFS household datasets, Spring quarters

nearly a third of the total, consisted of one adult of working age living on their own, including the single unemployed, the single disabled and the single divorced. Over a quarter were lone parent households, and once households with one adult past retirement age are counted, about two-thirds of workless households turn out to have just one adult of working age. It is the growth in such households that explains a large part of the apparent upward trend in workless households and it is the greater preponderance of such households in the UK that helps explain the relatively higher workless household rate when compared to other OECD countries.

About a third of workless households had dependent children, and a little under one in six children lived in a workless household in 2000. As worklessness is associated with high levels of poverty, the achievement of the objective of abolishing child poverty would have to rely heavily on a reduction in the proportion of workless households, or a significant improvement in the incomes of those households. The explicit target of securing 'A reduction in the number of children in workless households over the three years to 2004' might seem relatively easy to achieve in a tightening aggregate labour market. The number of children in workless households has been falling slowly and steadily since 1994-95. However, the target as it stands is consistent with either a further small fall or a big fall. This congruence between the employment and child poverty targets is discussed further below.

The apparent upward drift in the worklessness rate for households with children is explained in no small part by the growing proportion of lone parent households (Table 2.3). In Spring 2000 the proportion of two-adult households with children and without anyone in work was similar to the proportion in 1990. The proportion of lone parent

---

Table 2.3 Workless households as a percentage of all working-age households, by household type

	Couple with children	Lone parent	All with dependent children	All with dependent children (adjusted for increase in lone parent households)
1990	5.2	49.1	12.1	12.1
1992	8.7	53.6	16.1	15.8
1993	9.1	54.5	16.8	16.1
1994	9.0	54.0	17.3	16.0
1995	8.2	53.0	17.1	15.2
1996	8.0	51.6	17.2	14.9
1997	6.9	49.9	15.7	13.8
1998	6.6	48.5	15.7	13.4
1999	6.0	47.8	15.1	12.8
2000	5.5	44.8	13.9	11.7

Source: Labour Market Trends, January 2000 – LFS household datasets, Spring quarters

households without anyone in work had declined. Adjusting the proportion of all households with children that are workless for the increase in the importance of lone parent households (using a simple 'shift-share' analysis) removes all of the apparent upward trend.

In 2000 over two-thirds of workless households with dependent children were lone parent households, up from two-fifths in 1990. The problem of children growing up in workless households is thus overwhelmingly and increasingly the problem of relatively low employment rates among lone parents.

The want work rate

In Autumn 2000, along with 1.58 million people who were ILO unemployed, there were another 2.27 million who said that they wanted a job but were not looking for work or were not available to start and therefore did not count as ILO unemployed. Adding these two groups together would have given a 'want work' rate of 8.2 per cent (as a proportion of the adult population) compared with an ILO unemployment rate of 5.3 per cent.

Britain, along with Denmark, Austria and the Netherlands, has the highest proportion of its inactive saying they would like to work. The fact that those EU

Table 2.4 Movement out of worklessness and inactivity

	Proportion who became employed during the next 3 months	Number in category
	Average % 1993-99	Autumn 1999 (000s)
Unemployment		
Unemployed less than 6 months	34.6	954
Unemployed 6-12 months	23	258
Unemployed more than 12 months	11.3	493
Inactivity		
Searching for work, but unavailable to start	28.1	213
Discouraged (want a job but not searching because believe none available)	5.3	61
Wants a job but not searching for some other reason	7.1	2,011
Does not want a job	6.5	5,282

Source: Bank of England Inflation Report, February 2000

countries with the lowest unemployment rates and some of the best employment rates also have a higher proportion of the inactive saying they want to work is suggestive of an 'added worker' effect. The very fact of the better aggregate labour market in those countries may give a higher proportion of the inactive a reason to signal a somewhat closer attachment to the labour market.

However, how close is this attachment? If we look at the proportion of those in various categories of inactivity or unemployment who subsequently move into employment, the attachment to the labour market of most of those who 'want work' does not seem significantly higher than those amongst the inactive who say that they do not want a job (Table 2.4).

The only group that has transition rates into employment that match those of the ILO unemployed is the relatively small group who say that are searching for work but are unavailable to start. A significant proportion of this group consists of students. We may want to add this group to the ILO unemployed to get an idea of the active pool of job hunters. However, the 'want work' rate that is commonly quoted appears to lack an obvious labour market rationale if most of these people have very low transition rates into employment (and also uses the wrong denominator in calculation). Using the aggregate *employment* rate allows one to focus on policies to reduce economic inactivity across the board and allows for much fairer international comparisons.

Geographical disparities in unemployment

Unequal patterns of economic prosperity and employment have been a feature of the UK labour market for many decades. The debate over the correct spatial scale at which to analyse patterns of joblessness has also been raging for many years (see Webster 1999 and Gordon 1999). Is the region, the local authority district or the electoral ward the best unit of analysis? Employment rates within regions vary significantly. Concentrations of unemployment at ward level may reflect as much the operation of the housing market as the labour market. The Government prefers to use local authority districts as the basis for the setting of targets to reduce geographical disparities, but they often bear no obvious relationship with actual labour markets, particularly in urban areas.

Geographers and labour economists more often use the 'local labour market' or 'travel-to-work-area' (TTWA) as a basis for analysis. This would be consistent with much of the Government's analysis and its policy approach, which emphasises the importance of breaking down the supply side barriers that prevent people from accessing jobs within normal travel-to-work distance. However, a listing of TTWAs with low employment rates would emphasise that many are located some distance from any obviously 'booming' areas and thus pinpoint those localities where a demand side approach focussed on actual job generation was also required.

Claimant unemployment rates across the regions converged over the 1990s, thus potentially alleviating one of the structural problems within the UK labour market preventing aggregate unemployment from falling without generating inflation. However, the claimant unemployment rate understates regional disparities in joblessness, particularly because of the high levels of inactivity due to sickness and disability in the North of England, Wales and Scotland (Table 2.5). Including the sick and disabled would not alter the finding that jobless rates declined evenly in the 1990s across the regions. However, revisions by the ONS to data on regional GDP per head revealed a modest deterioration in regional imbalances in Britain over the period 1989-99.

Table 2.5 Claimants of key benefits by region, 1995-2000

	% of working age population			% in key categories, May 2000		
	1995	1997	2000	Unemployed	Sick & disabled	Lone parents
North East	24	22	20	4	12	3
Wales	23	22	20	3	13	3
North West	22	20	18	3	11	3
Scotland	21	20	18	4	11	3
London	21	18	15	4	7	4
West Midlands	18	16	15	3	8	2
York & Humber	18	17	15	3	9	3
East Midlands	16	14	13	3	8	2
South West	14	12	11	2	6	2
East	13	12	10	2	5	2
South East	12	10	9	2	5	2
Great Britain	18	16	14	3	8	3

Source: 5% sample of benefit claimants, DSS

A better focus for analysis of spatial variations in joblessness is the travel-to-work area. Employment rates can be estimated using the Labour Force Survey, though being based on a sample survey they have a sampling error of several percentage points. This in itself means that any ranking of local labour markets is strictly meaningless and the identification of, say, the bottom 30 labour markets with the lowest employment rates risks excluding some other localities with employment rates that are not statistically significantly different. These comments serve to illustrate the limitations of the LFS in looking at local patters of joblessness and even more so at looking at changes in employment over relatively short periods of time which in almost every case may be spurious because of their lack of statistical significance.

Table 2.6 shows the geographical pattern of the 68 local labour markets with employment rates below 70 per cent in 1999-2000. There is a heavy concentration in

West Wales and the Valleys and most of Northern Ireland and significant parts of central Scotland and the Highlands and Islands. Merseyside and much of the North East, parts of Yorkshire and Devon and Cornwall and a number of seaside towns also have employment rates below 70 per cent.

Table 2.6 Travel-to-work areas with employment rates below 70% by region, 1999-00

Wales – 19 areas			North West – 3 areas		
eg	Merthyr	61%	eg	Liverpool	62%
	Aberystwyth	62%		Wirral & Chester	68%
N. Ireland – 9 areas			Yorks & Humber – 5 areas		
eg	Strabane	46%	eg	Whitby	58%
	Enniskillen	60%		Sheffield & Rotherham	69%
Scotland – 14 areas			Devon & Cornwall – 7 areas		
eg	East Ayrshire	64%	eg	Newquay	61%
	Glasgow	65%		Penwith & Scilly Isles	66%
North East – 8 areas			Seaside – 3 areas		
eg	Hartlepool	62%	eg	Clacton	60%
	Middlesbrough	63%		Great Yarmouth	69%

Source: Labour Force Survey Local Area Database

A fundamental policy point is that by definition these local labour markets are highly self-contained in terms of travel-to-work patterns. Most are not located near to other areas with large and relatively tight labour markets. Their low employment rates reflect a fundamental shortage of jobs.

The Government's target aimed at narrowing the gap between the 30 local authority districts with the lowest employment rates and the overall employment rate uses an arbitrary number and the wrong unit of analysis. Moreover, it fails to reflect the problems created by the small sample sizes in the LFS. A better target would focus on raising employment rates in all travel-to-work areas to at least 70 per cent by 2010 or 2011. The later date would allow one to use the Census to track the attainment of this target. The Census is in many ways the only really reliable source for local area analysis of employment rates. Between 1981 and 1991, 39 TTWAs out of 322 displayed a fall in employment rates, including some major cities and areas with large localised employment losses, particularly associated with the rundown of the coal industry (Green and Owen, 1998).

Target groups with low levels of employment

Lone parents

In spring 2000 just over half of all lone parent households with dependent children were in employment (Table 2.3). This was higher than the employment rate in spring 1990. Employment rates for lone parents are more responsive to the economic cycle and trends in aggregate employment than might be expected. The employment rate for lone parent households fell by nearly six percentage points between 1990 and 1993 and rose by almost 10 percentage points between 1993 and 2000.

This experience in the 1990s is somewhat at odds with the trends reported by Holtermann *et al* (1999) for the period 1984-90 when employment rates for lone parents were flat. There are important compositional changes taking place amongst lone parents, with significant growth in the proportion of single mothers, but with the divorced and separated still the single biggest category. These compositional changes are important because single mothers have the lowest employment rates. However, comparing 1990 with 2000, employment rates rose for both main types of lone parents and the overall lone parent employment rate would have risen faster if adjusted for the changes in the composition of lone parents.

It is important therefore not to confuse the problem of lone parents having a low overall employment rate with the notion that those rates are somehow impervious to improvements in the aggregate labour market. It is still important to emphasise of course that employment rates for lone parents lag significantly behind employment rates for other parents. However, as already noted, the real significance of lone parents is that they account for two-thirds of all workless households with children.

The Treasury has set a target of increasing the proportion of lone parents in work to 70 per cent by 2010, which would be broadly comparable to lone parent employment rates in other countries. This would imply around an extra 230,000 lone parents in employment.

The over-50s

The sharp downward trend in employment rates for men over 50 from the late 1970s to the mid-1990s has been well documented (Campbell, 1999 and Performance and Innovation Unit 2000). As shown in Figure 2.3, in 1979, 84 per cent of men aged 50-64 were in employment. This proportion had fallen to 67 per cent by 1987 and after a modest recovery in the late 1980s fell further to 64 per cent by 1993.

Less well documented is the apparent end of that downward trend during the 1990s. Employment rates among men aged 50-64 improved at a faster rate after 1993 than the employment rate for men aged 25-49 or the overall employment rate. By 2000 employment rates for men aged 50-64 had recovered to the same level as in 1990.

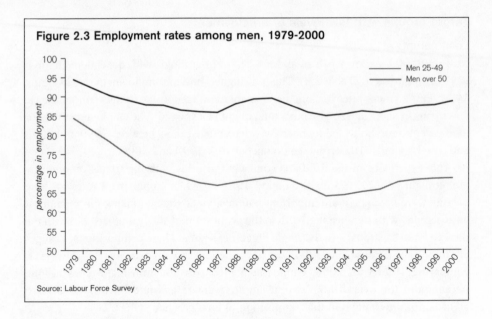

Figure 2.3 Employment rates among men, 1979-2000

Source: Labour Force Survey

In the 1990s then employment rates for older men have proved surprisingly responsive to the economic cycle and overall trends in the aggregate labour market, though of course they remain at historically low levels. One reason may be that many of the causes identified by the Performance and Innovation Unit as explaining the decline in labour force participation in the 1980s may be reversing:

- Structural changes in the economy and the labour market have slowed down (especially following the haemorrhage of manufacturing jobs in the early 1980s)

- Firms offering occupational pensions no longer have the same leeway to use those pensions to subsidise early retirement as fund surpluses run down.

- Public pensions policy is signalling a change in direction to discourage early retirement

- The government has introduced incentives to promote employment amongst the over-50s including a New Deal, aimed at reconnecting older adults to the labour market.

- Perhaps most importantly a tighter labour market is likely to alter the attitudes of employers to the over 50s as they struggle to recruit and retain labour

- A tighter labour market will also make discriminatory practices harder to sustain.

- Public policies aimed at countering age discrimination will reinforce the pressures from the labour market.

A key issue is whether these pressures will reduce exit from the labour market of those older workers currently employed, but be less successful in drawing back into the labour market those who have been inactive for long periods. Also at issue is how long this combination of factors may take to reverse the 'culture of early retirement' that some identify. A man currently in his mid-30s has a life expectancy of around 85 and a woman, 88. Retirement at 65 would still leave 20 or more years of time to enjoy the 'third age', but it is unclear whether expectations have yet to adjust to this reality.

If employment rates for men aged 50-64 were to recover to their levels in the late 1970s, that is from 69 per cent in 2000 to around 84 per cent, this would require an increase in employment of about three-quarters of a million. This would result in an increase in the aggregate employment rate of about two percentage points. This does not take into account any further rise in employment rates for women over 50, though the equalisation of the pension age would seem to imply this over the longer term.

Disabled people

Disabled people are far more likely than the non-disabled to be unemployed or economically inactive. However, precise measurement is impossible both because of the difficulty of defining disability, and because not all respondents to surveys are willing to talk about their health problems. It is also important to distinguish between disabled people in general and those entitled to disability benefits, which form the target group for welfare to work measures like the New Deal for the Disabled. Not all disabled people remain so permanently – over half who become limited in daily activities have spells lasting less than two years (Burchardt, 2000).

Using a current broad definition – including all those who report having either a current disability covered by the Disability Discrimination Act (DDA) or a work-limiting disability – there were 6.6 million people with long-term disabilities in the UK in winter 1999/2000. Only 46 per cent of them were in employment, compared to an employment rate of 80 per cent for the rest of the working age population. The ILO unemployment rate was also more than twice as high, at 10.8 per cent compared to 5.2 per cent for non-disabled people. There are significant regional variations in the prevalence of disability, with the highest levels in Wales and the North of England, the areas with the lowest employment levels (Table 2.5).

Gauging trends over time is complicated by changes in the wording and frequency of questions on the main official surveys such as the LFS. These have produced substantially different estimates for the total extent of disability in the population, as well as the economic activity rates of disabled people. Until 1993, the standard definition used in the LFS was based on a single question – respondents were asked if they had health problems that would affect any kind of paid work they might do. A question was then added to ask if this would be expected to last more than a year. This produced the 'LFS disabled' definition. The need to monitor the effects of the 1995 Disability Discrimination Act (DDA) produced further question changes in Spring 1997.

The disabled employment rate has moved with the economic cycle. Between 1984 and 1990, the employment rate for disabled people rose almost as much as for the population as a whole, increasing by five percentage points. Even allowing for discontinuities in the data, the recovery in employment seems to have been slower in the 1990s (Figure 2.4).

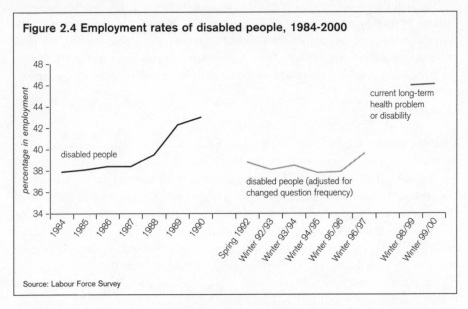

Figure 2.4 Employment rates of disabled people, 1984-2000

current long-term health problem or disability

disabled people

disabled people (adjusted for changed question frequency)

Source: Labour Force Survey

There has been a long-running trend for estimates of the prevalence of disability to rise on any definition, at least partly due to changing attitudes to and awareness of disability. This is likely to affect the level of employment as new people are included in the figures who might not previously have been counted. For example, the LFS question changes between 1996-7 and 1997-8 brought an increase in the proportion whose main health problem was 'back/neck problems' and 'depression/nerves'. Levels of economic activity vary considerably between different health problems, ranging from 70 per cent for hearing to 14 per cent for mental illness.

The number of people receiving benefit payments because they are unable to work on health grounds has increased significantly over the 1980s and 1990s. At the end of the 1990s around 1.6 million people were on Incapacity Benefit, roughly three times as many as 20 years ago. The number of people on long-term sickness benefit has also grown sharply. The extent to which this represents disguised unemployment is highly contested.

One million disabled people say they want to work, but as we have shown above, this is not necessarily a very useful measure of the potential labour supply. As a guide to the scale of inactivity, halving the difference in employment rates between disabled people and the total population (a rise in the employment rate to 60 per cent) would involve around an extra 900,000 people entering work, adding about 2.5 percentage points to the aggregate employment rate.

Ethnic minorities

Unemployment and employment rates for some ethnic minority groups have been described as 'super-cyclical'. That is unemployment/employment rates rise/fall especially steeply during recessions, but also tend to fall/rise somewhat faster during recoveries, a trend that has been observed since the 1970s.

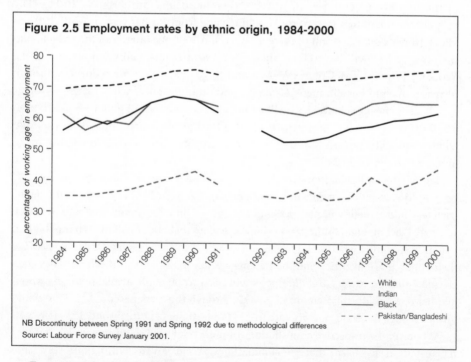

Figure 2.5 Employment rates by ethnic origin, 1984-2000

NB Discontinuity between Spring 1991 and Spring 1992 due to methodological differences
Source: Labour Force Survey January 2001.

For example during the period of economic recovery from 1984-90, the employment rate for black adults of working age rose by 10 percentage points and the employment differential with white adults narrowed. However, in the recession of

1990-93 employment rates for black adults fell by 13 percentage points, more than wiping out previous gains. Black workers suffered especially hard in the early 1990s recession because of their regional concentration in Greater London, which was hit particularly hard in that recession. Employment rate differentials have narrowed significantly since 1993, but the gap with the white population remains wider than in the late 1980s. Employment rates for Indian adults are less cyclically sensitive. Employment rates for the Pakistani and Bangladeshi community are especially low, reflecting in part very low economic activity rates amongst women.

If employment rates for ethnic minority groups matched those for the white population of working age, about an extra 400,000 people would be in work, adding about one percentage point to the aggregate employment rate.

Employment and the child poverty pledge

An analysis of the Government's attempts in this Parliament to reduce child poverty has confirmed that it is on track to secure a significant reduction of around one million in the number of children in poverty (Piachaud and Sutherland, 2001). The proportion of children in poverty should decline from 26 per cent in April 1997 to about 18 per cent as a result of current policies. About one quarter of the reduction in the poverty gap will have come about as a result of the minimum wage and the Working Families Tax Credit (WFTC) and three-quarters of the reduction through increases in child benefit, income support and other means tested benefits.

This significant achievement will come at a revenue cost of about £5.5 billion in 1999-00 prices or 0.6 per cent of GDP. One can of course infer from this that eliminating child poverty through further redistribution may cost something up to another two per cent of GDP.

For families with children over five the Government's aspiration is that parents will be able to gain employment. In-work benefits such as WFTC and universal benefits such as Child Benefit will play a significant role in boosting family incomes for those in work. Piachaud and Sutherland (2000) calculate that about half of all poor children live in households where the parents are assumed to be available for work, because their children are over five and the parents are not pensioners or disabled. They then calculate that an extra *1.5 million* jobs will need to be made available to take about another one million children out of poverty through the work-based route. This would further reduce the child poverty rate from about 20 per cent to around 12.5 per cent.

Whatever the respective contributions of the work-based route and straightforward redistribution, it is clear that the elimination of child poverty will require very large resources and a very large increase in employment. An extra 1.5 million jobs is equivalent to an increase in the aggregate employment rate of about four percentage points.

Policy conclusions

A focus on the low employment rates of key disadvantaged groups does suggest that the Government's headline target that by the end of the decade a higher percentage of people should be in employment than ever before is remarkably lacking in ambition. The 1974 peak in employment at 75.7 per cent of the working age population was only about one percentage point higher than the employment rate in Autumn 2000. The government's objectives of eliminating child poverty and tackling social exclusion through the promotion of employment would seem to demand a significantly higher target:

- Whatever the respective contributions of the work-based route and straightforward redistribution, it is clear that the elimination of child poverty will require a very large increase in employment. An extra 1.5 million jobs would be required if all parents who can work did. This would include those lone parents with children over 5 and would require an increase in the aggregate employment rate of about four percentage points.

- If employment rates for men aged 50-64 were to recover to their levels in the late 1970s this would require an increase in employment of about three-quarters of a million and an increase in the aggregate employment rate of about two percentage points.

- For the partly overlapping group of the disabled, halving the difference between the disabled and overall employment rates would mean an extra 900,000 jobs, adding 2.5 percentage points to the overall rate.

- If employment rates for ethnic minority groups matched those for the white population of working age, about an extra 400,000 people would be in work, adding one percentage point to the aggregate employment rate.

Overall then, significant inroads into economic inactivity and the promotion of employment amongst parents in order to reduce child poverty would require an increase in the employment rate to at least 80 per cent and probably higher. A target for the end of the decade of an employment rate of 80 per cent would signal the Government's acceptance of the scale of the challenge and would match the achievements of the best performing OECD countries.

True full employment would also have to include the whole country, not just the most prosperous regions. A target of raising employment in all travel-to-work areas to at least 70 per cent by 2010 would be a useful measure of this. An intermediate target for a national employment rate by 2004 at least two percentage points higher than the current rate, and a percentage point higher than the post-war peak would be a useful milestone. Along with a commitment to get the ILO unemployment rate down to 4 per cent and keep it there, the Government might then be able to claim fairly that it had achieved full employment.

References

Berstein J (1999) 'Benefits of full employment: Three lessons from the US economy' *New Economy* 6.3 Blackwell Publishers

Burchardt T (2000) *The Dynamics of being disabled* CASE Paper 36 London School of Economics

Campbell N (1999) *The Decline of Employment Among Older people in Britain* CASE Paper 19 London School of Economics

Department for Education and Employment (1999) *Employability and Jobs: Is there a jobs gap?* Memorandum by the DfEE to the Select Committee on Education and Employment, 1998-99 session.

Department for Education and Employment (2001) *Towards full employment in a modern society* Stationery Office

HM Treasury (2000) *2000 Spending Review: Public Service Agreements* Cm 4808.

Gregg P, Hansen K and Wadsworth J (1999) 'The rise of the workless household' in Gregg P and Wadsworth J (eds) *The State of Working Britain* Manchester University Press.

Gordon I (1999) 'Targeting a leaky bucket: the case against localised employment creation' *New Economy* 6.4 Blackwell Publishers

Green A and Owen D (1998) *Where are the jobless? Changing unemployment and non-employment in cities and regions* The Policy Press

Performance and Innovation Unit (2000) *Winning the Generation Game: Improving opportunities for people aged 50-65 in work and community activity* The Stationery Office

Piachaud D and Sutherland H (2001) *How Effective is the British Government's Attempt to reduce Child Poverty?* CASE Paper 38 London School of Economics

Piachaud D and Sutherland H (2000) 'Child Poverty – progress and prospects' *New Economy* 8.2 Blackwell Publishers

Webster D (1999) 'Targeted local jobs' *New Economy* 6.4 Blackwell Publishers

Appendix: Assessing the labour market performance of the Labour Government, 1997-2001

The Government has made much of the continued fall in unemployment and the increase in employment of over one million in the period since the May 1997 election. The obvious question to ask is how this performance compares with the equivalent period before the election?

	ILO unemployment	Claimant count unemployment	Total employment
Spring 1993	2,997	2,919	25,568
Spring 1997	2,087	1,673	26,916
Nov 2000 – Jan 2001	1,535	1,027	28,086
Source: Labour Market Trends			

Between Spring 1997 and the end of 2000 employment rose by 1,170,000, compared with a rise of 1,348,000 between Spring 1993 and Spring 1997. ILO unemployment fell by 550,000 between 1997-2000/01, compared with 910,000 between 1993-97. The claimant count fell by 646,000, 1997-2000/01, compared with 1,246,000, 1993-1997.

The picture then is of Labour inheriting an economy that had been generating steady increases in employment and of that steady improvement in aggregate employment continuing. Unemployment has edged down at a slower rate since the election. This is to be expected in a mature recovery when the authorities will wish to approach full employment at a more steady pace and where the tighter labour market will be attracting back some of the inactive so that given employment increases produce smaller falls in unemployment.

An objective outsider would identify a picture of 'steady as she goes' rather than any sea-change in labour market performance since 1997. Labour can be congratulated for successfully continuing the economic recovery and rise in employment, but they did not originate it.

There is one exception to the relatively smooth pattern of change over the period 1994-2000. In the period between September 1993 and June 1997, employment in manufacturing rose by 193,000. Between June 1997 and December 2000, employment in manufacturing declined by 342,000. This decline has of course been more than offset by increases in employment in other sectors. However, the fact remains that by having no policy to address the over-valued exchange rate inherited in 1997, the Labour Government has turned out to be rather bad for manufacturing jobs.

3. Globalisation, technology and the service economy: implications for job creation

Adair Turner

This chapter looks at the impact of technology on job creation. It does so within a discussion of how the overall shape of mature economies is changing, under the influence of three major forces: globalisation, technology and the rise of the service economy. The analysis is structured around two kinds of assertion about employment creation that have dominated discourse on this subject since the mid 1990s. They are the 'global economic threat' school of thought, and the new paradigm of the 'knowledge based economy'. They share some common underpinning theory, but while the second is more current and interesting, the first stems from almost total conceptual confusion.

Information and Communication Technology is going to destroy more jobs than it creates, but this does not matter. In this ICT intensive world, while it is certainly true that almost everyone will use ICT to some degree, many of the most rapidly growing jobs will be in some sense high-touch rather than high-tech. There will be more care workers, nursing staff, cooks, teachers, amusement park entertainers, sports centre professionals (and with the take-off of e-retailing, more scooter and delivery van drivers). This apparent paradox should not surprise us, because it is produced by changes in relative prices and productivity. Thanks to their greater potential for productivity improvements, IT based and traded goods and services tend to fall in price, offsetting the growth in their volume, while face-to face personal services (often inherently untradeable) tend to rise in relative price. ICT is thus self-limiting as a proportion of GDP – tending to increase over time the share of the economy accounted for by everything that we cannot automate, or do not want to.

The changing story

At any one time, policy debates on economics tend to be driven by dominant themes and assumptions about the major forces at work. The striking thing, looking back over the 1990s, is how rapidly and completely these change. At the beginning of the decade one dominant theme was the inherent superiority of stakeholder economies – Japanese and German manufacturing capability triumphant, more long-termist and investment oriented. The Anglo-Saxons had to change. In the mid-1990s it was all the Asian threat – relentless tides of global competition hitting the US and Europe from low cost, low income Asian tigers. We were told we had to rise to the challenge, cut costs or simply fade away – Europe in particular.

But then in 1997 Asia crashed. And suddenly numerous commentators sprang forth to explain that the Asian tigers, far from being paragons of free-market virtue, were in fact disaster zones of crony capitalism, lacking transparent accounting and sound corporate governance. They needed to change and become more free market and more like America. Then came Autumn 1998, with global financial volatility, and a global fear of credit crunch. The global financial markets had to change and presidents and prime ministers made thoughtful speeches about the need for a new world financial architecture.

But only 15 months later it all seemed like a bad dream. For suddenly we were not on the brink of an impending crisis, but marching joyously into a new economic paradigm – the paradigm of the net, of the dot.com – with productivity growth rising, inflation dangers dispelled, and the only relevant question 'don't you get it?' Only, in late 2000, for fashion to change again, with few people willing to own up to the extravagant claims they made so recently for the new economy.

At the very least that history should make us deeply suspicious of each new twist of economic fashion and committed to calibrating new developments and new assumptions with care, and to understand some of the long term trends which underlie these fluctuations in performance and belief.

As the overall story has changed so too have the specific assertions made about unemployment and about the relative success of different economies in creating employment.

The 'global economic threat'

The assertion popular in the mid 1990s saw employment creation and defence as above all about competitiveness in a fierce world of global competition. The world was seen as becoming relentlessly more global, with more and more sectors open to competition not just in goods but in services too; not just electronics from Taiwan but software and on-line reservation services from Bangalore. This competition from lower income and more competitive countries was seen to pose a threat to both prosperity and employment in the rich west, with high-paid American jobs taken over by Asian competitors and replaced by lower paid service jobs. A subset of this story was that Europe was uncompetitive, its costs too high, its public sector too large, its taxation too onerous, and suffering high unemployment because of this failure of competitiveness.

These propositions are largely nonsense, or as Paul Krugman (1996) has termed them 'Globaloney'. The whole concept of global competition between nations is deeply flawed. The world economy is not a zero-sum game in which some must win while others lose. Competitiveness is meaningless outside the specification of the exchange rate, which can and will move over time to offset imbalances in the external position. The only way that developments in international trade can lead, at least temporarily, to a fall in a country's national income is via adverse movements in the terms of trade, higher import prices relative to exports. This is the precise opposite of the falling import prices which concerned the devotees of the Asian competitiveness threat.

In fact the vast majority of economic activity in a rich developed economy is either internal to that economy or involves trade with other countries of a similar income level. Sixty two per cent of EU trade is intra-European and 16.5 per cent is with other rich countries – the US, Japan, Switzerland, Norway – leaving only six per cent of GDP traded with lower and middle income countries. This percentage is slightly down over the last 15 years and includes raw material flows such as oil. The growth in trade intensity, including intra-European, did indeed rise significantly between the early 1960s and early 1980s, but since then there has been no clear trend. It has risen in the last few years, but only to the level of 15 years ago (Figure 3.1).

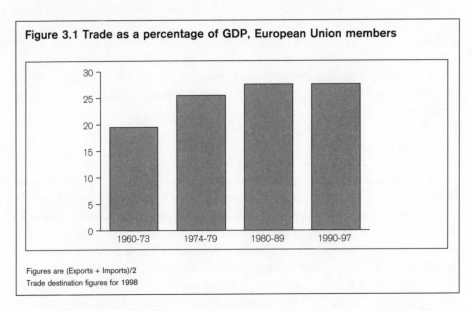

Figure 3.1 Trade as a percentage of GDP, European Union members

Figures are (Exports + Imports)/2
Trade destination figures for 1998

So the influence on developed countries of imports from low incomes is for empirical as well as theoretical reason, vastly more limited than writers like Lester Thurow have suggested. This sounds counter-intuitive to many people, though. We hear year by year of greater trade intensity in particular sectors – there really are more car parts from Egypt, more software services from India – and we also hear of trade volume growth well above GDP growth. That sounds like it means increasing trade intensity.

The explanation for this apparent paradox is that the impact of this growing intensity in some sectors is continually offset by the rise in the economic importance of non-traded service intensive sectors. These sectors, like restaurants and health care, education and sports centres, rise in importance at least partially because they are less susceptible to productivity growth and automation. The very factors which make goods and services inherently tradeable, also make them more inherently susceptible to rapid productivity growth and thus to relative price decline: and vice versa for untradeable sectors. In the 1980s and 90s, prices in the traded sector fell to an extent which almost exactly offset the effect of the growth in the volume of trade.

This also means that the idea that high European unemployment relative to the US can be meaningfully linked to a failure of competitiveness in simply mistaken. The supposedly uncompetitive European economies were throughout the 1990s running large current account surpluses. All of the employment rate difference between the EU and US is concentrated in services rather than manufacturing and within services primarily concentrated in untraded sectors such as health, education, retailing and wholesaling (Figure 3.2). High European unemployment in the 1990s is explained by a combination of low levels of domestic demand growth and more importantly by structural labour market features which have impeded the employment intensity of economic growth.

Figure 3.2 Share of employment and non-employment in USA and the EU

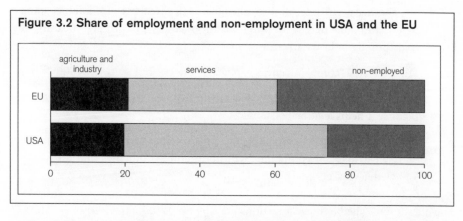

One key step in thinking about economic and employment creation performance is therefore to free our minds entirely from the confusions of 'globaloney'. This is not to deny the importance of some globalisation effects. The globalisation of competition within specific traded sectors is a vital factor for individual companies within many sectors. Globalisation of capital flows and idea flows, of best practice flows, is highly relevant in all sectors – non-traded as much as traded. It can be a major stimulus of accelerated structural change and productivity growth. Global short-term financial flows pose specific dangers which we would be unwise to assume have gone away.

But the idea of global competition between countries rather than between companies was a 1990s red herring, which we need to reject. For a country, external competition is not the fundamental challenge. Instead there are two fundamentals of economic success:

- achieving a high productivity growth rate in all sectors of the economy, traded or non-traded equally

- attaining a low rate of involuntary unemployment.

These two challenges are independent of any concept of external competitiveness and largely independent of one another. It is quite possible for a country to be good at one but poor on the other.

The knowledge based economy

The second set of assertions about economic performance and job creation are those linked to the knowledge based economy. The propositions advanced are that:

- changes in information and communication technology now in hand are not just another wave of technological change, but singularly profound, creating a new paradigm, increasing potential productivity growth significantly and transforming industry structures;

- Europe faces a competitiveness gap versus the US and must close it;

- while ICTs destroy jobs they also create them (a favourite with politicians because it helps legitimate change);

- this revolution affects all companies and has implications for all employees and skills, that 'all companies will be internet companies and all workers knowledge workers'.

The question of whether these assertions are true needs to be put into the context of what was really happening to mature economies and employment before about 1997, the year in which we all began to discover the new paradigm.

The growth of the service economy

What was happening above all was the growth of the service economy. 'Services' in the US for instance grew from 62 per cent of GDP in 1960 to 76 per cent in 1997, at the expense of manufacturing and agriculture. This is actually not a very useful statement, though, because 'services' thus widely defined cover a huge range of activities, including several which are not actually services, linked only by the fact that they are not manufacturing, nor construction, nor mining, nor agriculture.

The growth of the service economy in the US and Europe has been made up of three distinct elements. The first two are linked to shifts in consumer preference, the third unrelated though occurring at the same time. Firstly, as people get richer an increasing share of consumer demand tends to get focused on services not goods – more restaurant meals rather than washing machines. Secondly when richer people do buy physical goods an increasing proportion of the value lies in the design and branding and distribution and servicing and a decreasing proportion in the manufacture – a tendency deriving both from customer preference and from differential rates of productivity growth. Finally the service economy has grown as a result of the vertical disintegration of companies, with business functions in all sectors of the economy outsourced and subcontracted.

Looking both at income deciles and through time, richer people spend an increasing share of income on services rather than more physical goods. Since 1960 about 20 per cent of British household expenditure has shifted from goods to two categories of what national income accounts call services: services such as catering, transport, communication and tourism; and to the purchase or renting of housing (Figure 3.3).

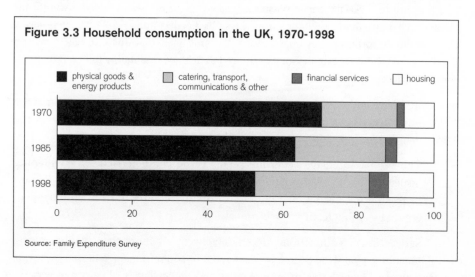

Figure 3.3 Household consumption in the UK, 1970-1998

Legend: physical goods & energy products | catering, transport, communications & other | financial services | housing

1970
1985
1998

0   20   40   60   80   100

Source: Family Expenditure Survey

This shift in consumer expenditure reflects partly an inherent hierarchy of consumer preferences (we reach satiation in washing machine consumption long before satiation in restaurant meals and health care consumption), but it also reflects the relative productivity and price effect described above. For example from 1980 to

1998 in Britain, durable goods demand in volume terms grew faster than real GDP at 140 per cent, and faster than catering at 77 per cent. But the price of durable goods grew only 62 per cent, catering services by 215 per cent. This made catering rise relative to durable goods as a percentage of GDP. Consumer expenditure and economic activity is continually shifting to the sectors where productivity growth is either more difficult to achieve or indeed most difficult to define.

The third element, vertical disintegration, is different in nature and in some senses less fundamental, even though its impact on measured labour force composition over the last ten years has been the most dramatic. Between 1988 and 1998, business services in the US grew from 6.5 to 9.4 per cent of total employment, creating four million new jobs and exceeding the growth of personal service related employment. However this growth did not reflect new customer demand for different goods and services, nor a shift of value along the value chain, nor indeed new activities for the individual workers involved. Instead it reflects outsourcing of a huge variety of business functions – computer processing and software development, market research and strategic planning activities, and security guards and catering and other building services. The biggest employment increase in any of the US Bureau of Labour Statistics' individual lines for those years is not a new set of economic activities but a new category of employment contract.

Whatever the consequences of the vertical disintegration effect, however, it is clear that the shift to a service and servicing intensive economy has involved a significant change in labour market composition, in skills needed and in relative incomes- a change with important policy implications. It seems likely that this shift has increased the degree of labour market flexibility required to achieve reasonably full employment. This is because:

- In service and servicing provision, unlike in goods, delivery has to occur at the time of customer demand, batching is less possible, and that increases the demand for part-time and temporary work

- The service intensive economy seems to be characterised by a widening dispersion in the relative labour productivity of different categories of labour, increasing the degree of wage rate flexibility required for full employment- especially at low income levels

- Service intensive functions are characterised, far more than manufacturing functions, by a wide degree of managerial freedom to make multiple trade-offs between higher levels of employment and higher levels of customer service. Extra people employed at the margin in a factory simply get in the way. Extra staff in a retail store or pub reduce your queue length or give you packed bags, delivering incremental service levels which customers value, but which do not have to be provided and which will not be provided if employment laws and wage fixing processes – all the panoply of different factors which determine the degree of labour market flexibility – are too restrictive.

For all these reasons, it seems likely that the move to a service intensive economy requires an increasing degree of labour market flexibility to achieve reasonable levels of unemployment. So one key cause of Europe's inferior employment performance in the 1980s and 1990s compared with the US, was not so much that Europe became more inflexible but that it failed to achieve the increases in flexibility required by changing economic structure. Europe's unemployment performance problem was concentrated exclusively in service sectors. More specifically Europe employs a far lower percentage of the working population in two key sectors; in hotels, restaurants and catering, retail, recreation, and in education, health and social work. The hypothesis applies very strongly for the former, and may also be true to a degree in the latter.

So the new paradigm arrived in a world where mature economies get ever-more service intensive, and where employment growth comes from the service sector, often in face-to-face activities. Europe's failure in the 1980s and 90s was that its growth was much less job intensive that the US, even though it was growing as fast in per capita terms, the corollary being faster productivity growth. Europe was doing better on the productivity challenge of economic success – the US at the employment creation challenge. Europe's job creation failure was to a significant degree explained by inadequate labour market flexibility to facilitate employment creation in the increasingly service and servicing intensive world. And then came along the 'new economy', the new paradigm which was meant to change everything. The question is – are the propositions of the knowledge based economy true, and what do they imply for employment?

The impact of ICT

There are indeed features about information and communications technology which are distinctive and which we would expect to have profound economic effects. The first is pervasiveness – ICT is not a technology relevant to only one particular industry or sector. It gets everywhere, potentially improving productivity and performance in almost every sector. That does not make it unique among technologies- electricity was similar. The combination with the second factor, however, is distinctive. This is the pace of technological advance. In ICT it is an order of magnitude, or ten times faster than the pace of the electrical mechanical revolution. Performance per price doubles every 18 months, possibly even faster in the last few years. The cost of computing per kilo bit of processing power will fall by about 98 per cent in the next ten years.

The third factor is particularly interesting to economists. ICT affects information processing and information exchange, and information plays a vital role in market economies. The relative efficiency of information flows within and between firms affects the optimal degree of vertical integration and the optimal size of firm. Change the economics of information exchange and we should expect big changes in industry structure. We can also expect significant changes in price searching and price fixing processes and in the relative economic power of different players in markets.

Finally, ICT has the potential to automate away activities which account for a large proportion of total economic activity. When you think about economic activity, it is clear that a huge proportion of it is actually involved not with the inherent activities required to deliver the goods or services customers actually value- but with monitoring and communication and meeting and administration, with placing orders and invoicing and accounting. These are all activities peculiarly susceptible to ICT based productivity improvements, and to the disappearance of which the consumer would be completely indifferent.

There are lots of these activities. McKinsey and Company estimated that 'interactive' activities in total add up to 51 per cent of total US GDP. This involves some heroic assumptions and highly debatable conceptual issues, but the key point is that it is very big. So we have a technology improving at a super-rapid pace addressing a huge slice of present economic activity – a formula for significant changes in economic and employment patterns.

The nature of this change is perhaps paradoxical to some devotees of this 'ever more knowledge intensive' economy. For the employment impact of technology change depends on a balance of two factors: the rapidity of technology change, and the extent to which the new technology generates new demand. Agricultural change in the 20th century combined rapid technological advance with minimal new demand creation, so its economic benefit derived from fewer people employed in it, and so freed up to do unrelated things. The automotive industry, at least until about 20 years ago was in a different category. New demand creation outstripped productivity improvement, increasing numbers of people employed in the world auto industry.

What will happen to ICT? We know it is very high on the rapidity of change dimension- the issue is where is it in terms of demand creation. Is it primarily a technology that simply automates away existing economic functions, freeing up resources to do other things? Or is it one that in and of itself directly creates new categories of consumer demand, that in a direct sense creates jobs as well as destroys them (Figure 3.4)?

It is certainly an industry growing in economic importance. US estimates suggest that all the ICT providing industries combined accounted for about 8.2 per cent of GDP in 1999, up from 5.8 per cent in 1990. These figures justify statements of the type that while ICT is still less than 10 per cent of GDP it is a quarter or a third of the increase in GDP.

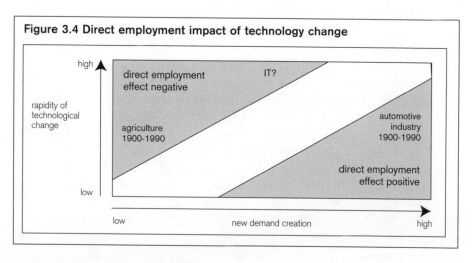

Figure 3.4 Direct employment impact of technology change

However, to a huge extent this activity is about improving the efficiency of existing economic functions rather than delivering new customer values. ICT was calculated to be 43.6 per cent of US plant and equipment investment at the end of the 1990s. Almost half of all business investment, the fundamental motor of productivity improvement, is about improved information and communications hardware and software. Turning to the consumption side, however, only 2.4 per cent of total personal consumption is spent on the consumer products and services of the ICT industry – all the mobile phone hardware and services, PCs and software, all the internet connections and usage. So far ICT is a huge event in business investment but in the total scheme of things a relatively small one in individual consumption patterns. That balance will have big consequences for where jobs are going to come from.

On the investment side, the issue is whether all this investment is going to deliver the productivity improvements which the inherent nature of this technology would lead us to expect. After all ICT investment has been running high as a percentage of total investment for many years. Indeed the big ramp up in spending was in the 1970s, not the 1990s. After a long time when 'IT is everywhere except in the productivity statistics' (as Robert Solow put it), it seems a reasonable inference that sustainable productivity growth has increased somewhat for at least a number of years. This does not mean the laws of economics have been dispelled, it is not the end for ever for inflation, but perhaps a ten year period in which sustainable productivity growth may be perhaps 0.5 per cent higher than we saw in the 1980s.

There are three possible reasons why this is occurring now and not in the 1980s. Firstly we are buying more and more ICT *capability*. The percentage of total investment may not have risen much, but for each dollar spent we are getting immensely more capability, cutting the cost and lead time of new investment. Secondly, this ICT now includes a larger element of 'C' – communications, including but not limited to the web itself, creating opportunities for process redesign between companies and sites rather than just within them. Thirdly, as a spin-off from the outsourcing and sub-contracting wave mentioned above, an army of professional subcontractors now serve many companies rather than being employed as middle managers jealously guarding company secrets, and so act as a powerful force for the accelerated transfer of best practice between them.

For these reasons the productivity spurt does seem for real, and a half per cent rise for 10 years seems a sensible mid point between over-cautious doubters and true religious believers. This does not imply that we will all become either intense ICT consumers or all become ICT workers. Given the 18-month rule, it is quite possible that in 20 years time consumers will consume 10,000 times as much computing and communications power as today, but it is also quite possible that the economic value of that power will have fallen not risen relative to the economic value of the world restaurant business.

This productivity effect has implications for employment. While America's ICT industries contribute 8.2 per cent of GDP in 1998, they only provided 3.7 per cent of employment. Running a mobile phone company does not take many people. Neither does running a software company, even if everybody in the world buys your product, because software reproduction is close to costless. This means that huge volume increases will often be accompanied with only minimal employment creation.

This does not deny some employment creation in ICT specific industries. The US Bureau of Labour Statistics forecast that the 3.7 per cent will grow to 4.8 per cent by 2008, but this is still under 5 per cent, and thereafter they may even begin to fall. Meanwhile, in the half of the economy made up of 'interactive' activities, huge numbers of employees are likely to lose their existing jobs, the inevitable consequence of the accelerated productivity growth.

So ICT is going to destroy more jobs than it creates. But the good news is that it does not matter, because a technology does not need to create jobs directly as well as destroying them to be economically beneficial. The agricultural revolution destroyed jobs but the people unemployed as a result found other jobs in completely unrelated areas of the economy. This is what will happen with the ICT revolution. ICT will automate away huge numbers of jobs, but provided labour markets are reasonably flexible, provided nominal demand growth is kept steady and adequate, and major unnecessary demand shock are avoided, new jobs will be created. They will most likely come from a continuation of the trend to service and servicing intensity that has been at work for the last several decades.

The US Bureau of Labour Statistics forecast for the next decade shows new jobs coming from the following combination of sources: 1.9 million in computer and data processing; 2.75 million from other categories of business services (of which over one million are 'personnel supply services' a continuation of the outsourcing trend but not a change in what work people do); 4.5 million more in restaurants and amusement centres and auto hire and cleaning and other personal services; and the biggest Figure of all – 4.95 million from more education and health and residential care – more nurses, teachers and care workers. These are just forecasts, but they fit the existing trends, what we know about the fundamental economics, and they are highly likely to be at least directionally correct.

This apparent paradox of an ICT intensive world, where almost everyone uses ICT to some degree, but where many of the most rapidly growing jobs are high-touch rather than high tech should not surprise us. It is just another example of the relative productivity growth/relative price factor which has been described several times in this chapter.

Conclusion and policy implications

These conclusion and hypotheses are prompted by the above analysis, but certainly not proven by it. They should help provoke thought on where the real problems of public policy lie and where they do not.

Policy issues we should not worry about

- *Job creation*

  There is no inherent problem of job creation, there is no lump of labour, and it does not matter that ICT destroys more jobs than it creates because other jobs will emerge. At one level and in the long term this is almost axiomatic and also not very helpful. It matters crucially how long the long term is and how smooth the transition. Agricultural jobs after all were fully replaced eventually, but only with some big social upheavals on the way.

  The more extreme and interesting version of this hypothesis is that the specific transition in employment we now face will be quite smooth, because transitional structural unemployment is reducing in importance as a problem for two reasons. First because one by-product of the shift to the service economy is that we no longer face the large regional concentrations and industry specific concentrations of employment and skill which used to exist. We have no equivalent of 750,000 miners in 1950 concentrated in specific regions where they accounted for a very high percentage of the regional workforce. Secondly because the ICT job shakeout is not in turn concentrated in one specific sector or region but is pervasive across the whole economy. We will have a big shakeout and big job creation, but a relatively smooth transition with less inherent mismatches than in previous major technological shocks.

- *Europe's competitiveness*

  Europe's big problem remains labour market flexibility and neither productivity nor competitiveness. Europe is a few years behind the US in the ICT revolution- but we should not worry about it at the level of public policy. There are powerful private forces acting to limit the size of the gap, there is an army of entrepreneurs looking to seize ICT opportunities, and because globalisation has created immensely effective mechanisms for the rapid transfer of best practice, including the transfer to Europe, within at most a few years, of every internet or other ICT idea launched in the US. Europe will gain the productivity boost from the ICT revolution; the open issue is whether it will free up labour markets fast enough to create new service sector jobs at the pace required.

- *The macro economy*

  'It's not the economy stupid'. The classical problems of overall growth and inflation and employment trends, though of course still important, are not the difficult issues of public policy. There are exceptions: you can still get macro-policy wrong if you follow silly policies – as in Japan – and asset price bubbles and short-term financial market volatility remain important dangers to stability. But in general Macro issues are less pressing than before.

Issues we will need to worry about

- *The growth of education and health expenditure*

  Health spending keeps rising in the US, and education was a key driver of employment growth. Richer people want to spend a higher percentage of their income on health and education, but if these are primarily publicly provided, that desire can come up against the countervailing desire to hold down taxes.

- *Inequality*

  There is not a problem of job creation, but there may be a problem of the income levels at which new jobs are created, because both the rise of the service economy and ICT may be forces significantly increasing income inequality. It is notable that while employment in the ICT industries is only increasingly slightly, those jobs are not only much better paid, but have incomes increasing faster than the average.

  The standard response, 'let us equip everyone with ICT skills' will not provide an adequate answer, even though it is certainly a good idea. Employability may be a function of absolute level of skills, but income distribution will often reflect relative skills, and the incremental value of higher relative skills seems for a variety of reasons to be increasing significantly.

This chapter was adapted from a lecture given at the LSE in March 2000

References

European Commission (1999) *Employment in Europe*

Krugman P (1996) *Pop internationalism* MIT Press

Thurow L (1992) *Head to Head: The Coming Economic Battle Among Japan, Europe and America* New York: Wm Morrow & Co

US Bureau of Labour Statistics (1999) *Statistical Abstract of the US 1999*

4. New technology and demanding jobs
Francis Green

> Freedom to work in a new way...Colleagues can work as a team even when
> they are miles apart, and share information as easily when they are out and
> about, as sitting at a desk. It gives people the flexibility to work wherever,
> whenever and however they choose. To find out how your business can
> take-off in ways that have never been possible before, call ...
>
> Advertisement for Orange Wirefree Working, *Guardian* 4.9.00.

Like many freedoms the 'freedom to work in a new way', exemplified in the above
commercial as a selling feature of mobile phone networks, comes laden with
obligations. It is a contradictory phenomenon that re-creates the age-old paradox, that
technology, which on the face of it should free up time for enjoyment, can sometimes
do the opposite. In the case of much new technology, the obligation accompanying the
new freedom appears to be the need to work in a more 'demanding' way.

That jobs have become more demanding is reported time and again by employers,
though exactly what that means is usually somewhat fuzzy. The commonest
interpretation is that required skill levels are rising, and there is ample statistical
evidence for this. An additional meaning of 'demanding', however, is that jobs are
requiring people to work harder than before. Some new evidence on work intensity
also supports this interpretation.

The importance of increasing skill requirements, both for researchers and for
policy-makers, is widely understood. The importance of excessive work hours has
been partially recognised through the introduction of the European Directive on
Working Time. The importance of work intensification has, however, had little impact
on researchers (largely because of difficulties of quantifying it), and virtually no impact
on policy. Its chief impact has been to help stimulate a growing industry of
occupational stress analysts and counsellors.

This chapter focuses on the twin changes that appear to be encompassed in the
phrase 'more demanding jobs', and brings out the links between them and with new
technologies. Firstly it summarises the factual case that jobs in Britain do now require
the labour force to be both harder working and more skilled. It then examines what
underlies these changes, and considers their links with new technology, as far as
current research appears to be revealing. Finally, some broad implications for
individuals, employers and government are discussed.

The facts about increasing work pressure[1]

A sense of increasing work pressure has pervaded public discussion of the workplace for several years. Since there is a deal of ill-informed hype about in this area, it is worth setting the statistical record straight on the key indicators of work pressure: the time spent at work and the intensity of work.

Work hours

With respect to hours of work, including those extra hours that are put in but not necessarily paid for, we have a reasonably good measure from the nationally representative Labour Force Surveys since the 1970s. What they tell us contradicts the notion that *on average* people were working increased hours in the last part of the 20th century. For the last two decades, average hours a week hovered around the 37 mark for the whole period (Figure 4.1).

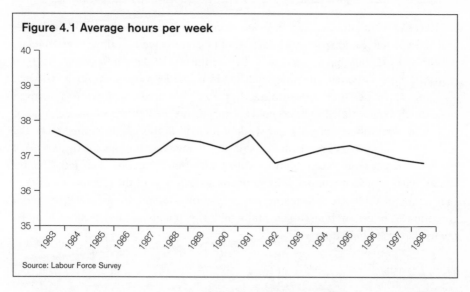

Figure 4.1 Average hours per week

Source: Labour Force Survey

A common error is to claim that UK citizens work the longest hours in Europe; in fact, average hours in Britain come somewhere in the middle of the range. Britain only comes top if the focus is on men. In contrast, women's average hours are among the lowest in Europe (Office for National Statistics, 1998). To summarise workers' hours by men's hours is both incorrect and sexist.

The idea that work pressure has increased is not reflected in this, the most obvious single statistic about weekly hours. What is happening?

It is more likely that the widespread sense of rising work pressure is linked partly to

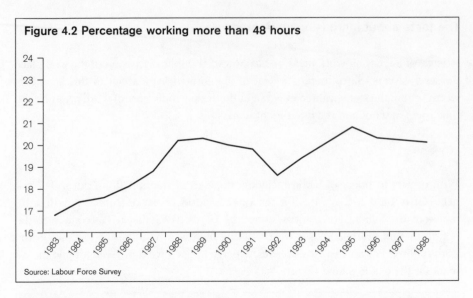

Figure 4.2 Percentage working more than 48 hours

Source: Labour Force Survey

the fact that, within this average, there are more people (of both sexes) working longer *and* more people working shorter hours. About one in six were working over 48 hours a week in 1981, but this rose to one in five by the end of the 1990s (Figure 4.2) – a palpable, if not a dramatic, increase, matched by a parallel rise in short-hours working.

Even more pertinent, the hours that were being worked were becoming increasingly concentrated in households. Thus, the average two-adult household put in an extra seven hours of work per week at the end of the 1990s, compared to the early 1980s (Figure 4.3); meanwhile, there were many more households by the end of the 1990s where there was nobody in work at all – more than one in six (see Chapter 2). So, what we can say about work hours as an indicator of the pressure of work is that although these are not getting any worse on average, they are getting more concentrated in certain households; and a minority, mainly but not exclusively male, are working very long hours.

Work intensity

Work intensity is much more difficult to measure. One way to do so is to use the subjective reports of people at work. It is easy to be sceptical about self-reports: individuals can deceive themselves, as well as others, about their lives, including their jobs. Nevertheless, when individuals are asked questions about their pace of work, they are likely to respond relative to some sense of what is a normal pace of work. There is evidence that individuals tend to understand questions about work effort, and that their qualitative responses are reliable (for a review, see for example, Green and Mcintosh, 1997).

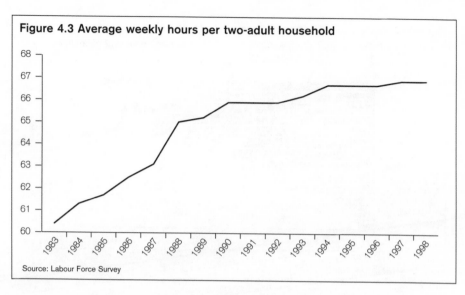

Figure 4.3 Average weekly hours per two-adult household

Source: Labour Force Survey

Recent survey evidence confirms unequivocally that there has indeed been an intensification of work effort in Britain in the last two decades (Green, 2001). Between 1992 and 1997, the proportion of workers strongly agreeing that 'My job requires that I work very hard' rose from 32 to 40 per cent (Figure 4.4). Assuming that workers were judging their work pace by the same standards in both years, this is reasonably good evidence of an intensification of labour. The figure shows that the intensification happened for both sexes, but more for women than for men.

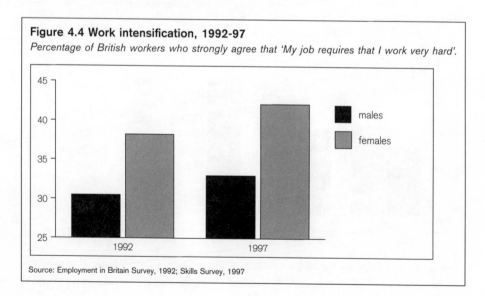

Figure 4.4 Work intensification, 1992-97

Percentage of British workers who strongly agree that 'My job requires that I work very hard'.

males

females

Source: Employment in Britain Survey, 1992; Skills Survey, 1997

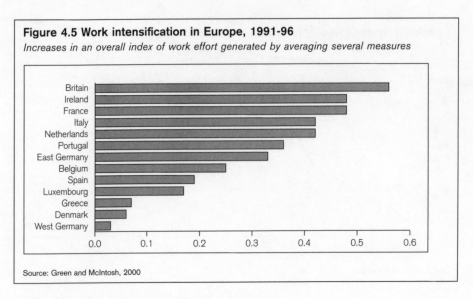

Figure 4.5 Work intensification in Europe, 1991-96

Increases in an overall index of work effort generated by averaging several measures

Source: Green and McIntosh, 2000

Survey evidence for 1991 and 1996 shows that the rise in work intensity was faster in Britain than in other European countries. For example, the proportions that reported working at very high speed 'all' or 'almost all' of the time rose from 17 to 25 per cent. Figure 4.5 shows increases in an overall index of work effort generated by averaging several measures (Green and McIntosh, 2000). As the graph shows, in certain countries – West Germany, Greece and Denmark, there was virtually no change in work intensity over the period.

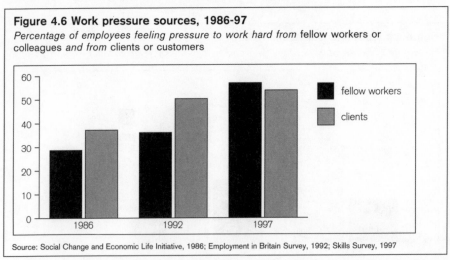

Figure 4.6 Work pressure sources, 1986-97

Percentage of employees feeling pressure to work hard from fellow workers or colleagues *and from* clients or customers

Source: Social Change and Economic Life Initiative, 1986; Employment in Britain Survey, 1992; Skills Survey, 1997

A third item to note concerns a measure of the pressure to work hard. Respondents to British surveys in 1986 and 1997 were asked to tick the factors on a list that influenced them to work hard. The respondents to the 1997 survey on average ticked off more items than did respondents to the 1986 survey, indicating that they felt more sources of work pressure (Figure 4.6) The proportions of respondents that ticked the influence of fellow workers: nearly doubled from 29 to 57 per cent. The influence of clients as a source of work pressure showed a not-quite-so-spectacular rise, but nevertheless remarkable.

These average statistics, drawn from successive representative surveys of Britain, are just some of a larger body of evidence confirming that this has been an era of work intensification (Green, 2001).

The facts about increasing work skills

The proposition that jobs are increasingly demanding higher levels of skills is hardly controversial. However, it is worth briefly restating the evidence because it must be remembered that increasing job skills is not an inevitable trend and that it need not continue. Although the average qualifications base of the workforce has risen steadily, this does not mean that jobs themselves are becoming more skilled. It could be that more people are becoming overqualified for their jobs.

One way of indicating rising job skills is through the declining proportions of jobs in lower-skilled occupations. Thus, the proportions of UK workers who were Process, Plant and Machine Operators or in Elementary Occupations fell from 30 per cent in 1981 to 23 per cent in 1998; meanwhile the proportions that were Managers and Senior Officials rose from ten per cent to 13 per cent (DfEE, 2000).

However, changes in occupational composition understate the rising skill because each occupation has tended to become more skilled. There is evidence of increasing demand for many key skills, and a substantial balance of workers report experiencing increases in their skills (DfEE, 2000). Figures 4.7 and 4.8 present more measures of

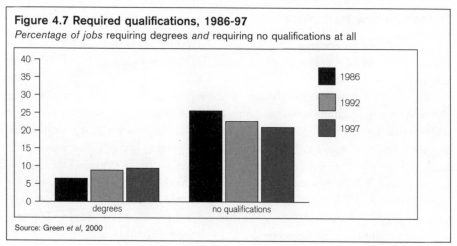

Figure 4.7 Required qualifications, 1986-97

Percentage of jobs requiring degrees *and* requiring no qualifications at all

Source: Green *et al*, 2000

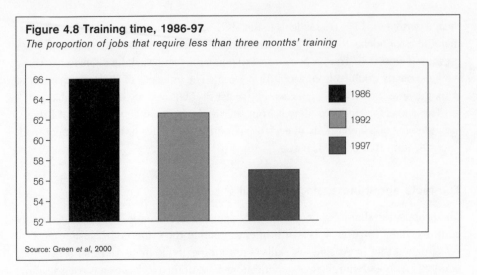

Figure 4.8 Training time, 1986-97
The proportion of jobs that require less than three months' training

Source: Green *et al*, 2000

rising job skills, taken from Green *et al*, (2000). These analyses are based on comparing responses to identical questions in surveys carried out in 1986, 1992 and 1997. Figure 4.7 shows that an increasing proportion of employment is in jobs that would require any new applicant to have a degree; a decreasing proportion is in jobs that could be obtained by people with no qualifications. Figure 4.8 shows the decreasing proportions of jobs where the worker requires less than three months training for that type of work. Another indicator is that a decreasing proportion of jobs take less than a month to learn (the presumption being that complex jobs require longer to learn).

Taken together, these indicators provide strong evidence that on the whole jobs in Britain really do require more skills than two decades ago.

The role of new technology

The role of new technology, and in particular information technology, has been central to the trend towards more 'demanding' jobs, both more skilled and more effort-intensive.

The most direct way in which new technology might be thought of as requiring higher skills is through the assumption that information processing is intimately linked with knowledge. In modern jargon, the modern skilled worker is the 'knowledge worker', and it is frequently claimed by management writers that knowledge management is the key to competitive success in the global economy. Correspondingly, 'symbolic' work, to use the phrase of ex-US Secretary of State for Labor Robert Reich, is the key to success in the global labour market (Reich, 1993). Consistent with this view, evidence in Britain and elsewhere shows a strong and significant relationship between computer use at work and skill levels.

Even after allowing for a multitude of other factors, it is found that individuals that use computers are in jobs which generally require higher skills; and firms which invest more in computers tend to employ higher skilled workers on average (Haskell and Heden, 1999). Indeed the relationship at the individual level is very strong, to the extent that just about all the upskilling that took place between 1986 and 1997 is associated with increasing uptake of computers by individuals at work (Green, Felstead and Gallie, 2000). This finding does not necessarily mean that computers were somehow causing people to become more skilled, though no doubt people do become more skilled through practical experience of computer use. Rather, it simply means that computers were being especially used in those jobs whose general skill levels were being raised in this period.

Yet it is likely that looking at individuals' computer use understates the true influence of information technology on skills demand. According to Timothy Bresnahan of Stanford University, the role of the PC in generating new skills demands is relatively limited. Instead, he argues that computer use has generated higher average skills demands through two main routes (Bresnahan, 1999).

First, it is the relatively low-skilled tasks that have proved most easy to automate. Clerical and related white-collar work has been radically transformed by the new technology, as computer decision-making arrives to substitute for human decision-making. The telephone operator jobs are at once less numerous (because call routing and other routine functions are now the job of the system), more complex and more pressured. Whole bureaucracies have been rationalised, thus dispensing with lower-skilled bureaucratic workers, transforming the lives of both back office and front office workers.

The second route to higher skills is via the links between technology and work organisation. The increasing sophistication of new technology enabled new forms of work organisation to be introduced that facilitated expansions in the efficiency of the labour process. Moreover, computer-based research began to transform the marketing function, enabling managers to fashion new services that more closely met customers wants. The imagination and the cognitive skills needed to find these new uses of the technology constituted a new set of managerial skills. Along with growing communication and social skills, necessary to introduce the necessary changes in work organisation, this meant an increasing demand for skill from managers in particular, and also from those further down the hierarchy. In short, the key to the role of information technology in generating new skills is the complementarity between changes in the technology and the associated changes in organisations.

The growth of team working, and the spread of Total Quality Management and Just-In-Time working, have been described by observers as having the effect of optimising the flow of work to workers. Thus, whereas before these innovations there were many occasions during the working day when people could slack off a bit, reduce concentration, and even have a break, such interruptions have now been reduced. The imperative of Total Quality Management is that many more individuals have to take continued responsibility for quality checks and improvements and so on. Rather than wait for someone to tell them what to do, they have to get on and do it. Multi-skilling, another widespread trend, also facilitates this closing-up of previously intractable time gaps.

Both the changes in work processes and the changes in work organisation are complemented by the development of ICT. Perhaps the most well-known example here is the call centre, the fastest-growing workplace of the last few years, now with over 400,000 workers in Britain. One distinguishing feature of call centre technology is the facility to deliver the next call instantaneously to each workstation, thus eliminating all gaps in the working day, except those that are explicitly negotiated. Typically, negotiated gaps for refreshments and so on are also subtracted from total working time when calculating pay. Call centre technology also has other features that help to ensure a high work intensity, such as the ability to monitor very closely the performance of each worker. However, I believe that the facility to optimise workflow is likely to be the crucial factor that intensifies the work.

Away from the call centre, ICT has analogous functions in jobs that allow much more autonomy for workers. An obvious example is the e-mail, which offers the possibility of rapid response and hence rapid communication, as long as communicants are willing to put in the appropriate effort. Along with the mobile phone, such modern technologies allow a much greater use to be made of work time, and also to extend out of the traditional workplace and into supposedly non-work hours. Again, the effect is to fill up gaps that would otherwise have been natural breaks in the pattern of work.

These developments could be described as a process of 'effort-biased technical change', meaning that the way technology has changed is to enhance the productivity of especially those workers who are able and prepared to put in high levels of effort. This is a parallel process to the more familiar 'skill-biased technical change' which raises the demand for higher skilled labour.

The consensus of economists is that the last part of the twentieth century was an era of skill-biased technical change. Is there any evidence for it being also an era of effort-biased technical change? The answer is a qualified yes.

In the 1998 Workplace Employee Relations Survey, which encompasses all sectors of the economy, it is possible to compare managers' judgements as to whether work has been intensified at the establishment with the introduction of new technology and work organisation. Where the establishment had introduced new technology in the previous 5 years, some 42 per cent of workplaces had experienced a substantial increase in the pace of work; but where no new technology had been introduced, the proportion was much less at 31 per cent. Similarly, where the establishment had introduced organisational changes, 45 per cent reported a substantial work intensification, compared to just 29 per cent for establishments with no changes in work organisation.

The hypothesis of effort-biased technological change does not, of course, constitute the whole of the story about why work has been intensified in Britain. Why people should consent to put in higher levels of effort is also of interest. If production line work becomes more intensive, many workers could in the long term look elsewhere for more congenial jobs but often do not do so. It is sometimes said, casually, that the machine itself is the cause: if the phone rings, it must be responded to; if the e-mail sits on your screen, you must reply to it.

However, that perspective misses the social context of the employment relationship. Many have argued that a crucial factor is the extent that employees are allowed to participate in decision-making at the workplace, thus becoming involved and at least partly committed to the firm that they work for. That commitment is reinforced by the growing tendency to tie pay in some way to performance. In 1998 nearly a third of establishments with at least 10 workers reported that an increasing proportion of pay had been linked to performance.[2] It is likely that information technology also plays an important role here, through enabling more accurate measurement of individual and team performance, and thus facilitating performance related pay in circumstances where it was previously not workable.

At the same time trade union influence has declined, and the fact that it has declined faster in Britain than elsewhere is closely associated with the relatively high level of work intensification in Britain compared to a number of other European Union countries (Green and Mcintosh, 2000). The obvious conclusion is that, to some extent, unions have in the past formed a barrier limiting the encroachments on workers' time. That barrier is now largely removed for the large majority of the economy. A further factor in Britain is the long-term retrenchment of public sector employment, and the progressive introduction of quasi-market institutions and incentives in the National Health Service, the civil service, local government and the education sector. Pay in these areas, relative to the national average, has declined at the same time as their effort has been intensified more than elsewhere. Those working in education report the highest levels of work intensification.

Although these other factors leading to work intensification are relevant, they do not detract from the importance of technology as a key source of work intensification. The evidence is convincing because it comes from a large, representative, high-quality survey of establishments. The only reservation is that the nature of the changes in technology and in work organisation are not specified in sufficient detail to pick up precisely the sorts of factors mentioned above.

Effort biased technological change and upskilling

So far two formally separate processes of effort-biased and skill-biased technological (or organisational) changes have been described. There is no inevitable reason for jobs that become more skilled to also become more intense, but in the recent era the two are closely linked. The first empirical discovery of a link between upskilling and work intensification, in the current era, was the finding by Duncan Gallie and Michael White that workers who reported experiencing increases in the skill requirements of their jobs were much more likely also to experience work intensification (Gallie and White, 1993).

Thus, the rise of skills in the early 1990s appeared to be coming at a cost of increasing 'work strain'. This trade-off is in contrast to the era of work intensification earlier this century that accompanied the spread of Taylorism and scientific management in the United States and later in Europe. Then, the intensification accompanied a systematic deskilling of craft labour (Braverman, 1974).

The factors that are now generating effort-biased technical change are likely to be associated with upskilling for several reasons. First and foremost, to the extent that information technology is the stimulus for change at work, we have seen how this generates demands both for higher skills and for greater effort. Second, a prime facilitating factor for effort-biased change is an increase in the flexibility with which managers can deploy workers to tasks, and in the associated multi-skilling of workers, which is likely to be associated with a more educated workforce. Third, the re-organisation of work more on the basis of teams goes hand in hand with a delayering of management hierarchies, increased devolution of responsibilities and increased discretion over work tasks for a sizeable proportion of the company's workforce. The exercise of discretion requires a certain level of self-motivation, at least in the short term, to ensure compliance with the firm's requirements. At the same time, increased discretion over work methods entails better knowledge of the overall production process, and thus higher levels of skills. Thus high and fairly stringent effort norms are complementary with jobs that entail large amounts of discretion and hence skill.

There is a further sense in which greater motivation is often associated with higher skill, namely through the ambiguities in the notion of skill itself. To the dismay of psychologists and economists, a widespread phenomenon is for employers to see certain employer-favouring attitudes, or qualities such as reliability or honesty, as skills. Reported skill shortages are known to refer frequently to shortages of reliable people who can fit in, rather than to technically skilled personnel (Oliver and Turton, 1982). Faced with multiple stressors, those who get by are said to have 'coping skills'.[3] And a sizeable minority of employers who sponsor training do so in order partly to generate enthusiasm for corporate objectives (Felstead, Green and Mayhew,

1997). In short, if skill is interpreted to include such personal attributes and attitudes, skill-biased change is ipso facto also an effort-biased change.

Policy implications

The present government's stance towards the promotion of new technology has been generally supportive and enthusiastic, aiming to harness it for the goal of social inclusion, promote it in schools. Yet if jobs are becoming more 'demanding', at least in part on account of new technologies, how if at all should government or other collective institutions respond?

Skills matching

Most obviously, the increased demand for skills deriving from new technologies implies that there is a need for education and training institutions to respond accordingly. The role of the state in this respect has been very widely aired (see e.g. Stevens, 1999). However, it is worth emphasising the importance of attempts to match skill supply to demand. From an economic perspective, investing in qualifications that are never used in the workplace is wasteful and can generate significant dissatisfaction with jobs. Education not connected to work is absolutely fine, but care needs to be taken not to generate false expectations about work.

Since skill changes are long-term, there is a strong need for a strategic and encompassing perspective when planning education and training policy. Setting up the National Skills Task Force was a step in the right direction. Public support for new information and communication technologies needs to be maintained, especially through strategic planning of skills supply to match needs over the long-term. The National Skills Taskforce has made recommendations in this respect. It remains to be seen whether the new institutional arrangements of Learning and Skill Councils, working with the Regional Development Agencies, will be able to generate an ongoing strategic approach to developing Britain's ICT skill supply.

Work intensification and productivity growth

But what of the implications of the work intensification that appears to accompany modern-day technologies? Does the harder work imply greater productivity, and if so is that productivity growth sustainable? Can individuals choose their effort levels, and if so why should government intervene?

Evidence at the sectoral level suggests that harder work is indeed rewarded with greater productivity. Thus, in the 1980s, the manufacturing sector had a level of work intensification significantly higher than the average. Simultaneously, it experienced a high rate of productivity growth (driven more by employment reductions than by output growth) while having very low levels of net investment. The productivity growth arose mainly through some combination of harder work by remaining employees and improved efficiency (O'Mahoney, 1994; Evans, Ewing and Nolan, 1992). In the 1990s, work intensification was highest, by contrast, in the education sector. While there are no national accounting figures to reflect it, productivity in this non-market sector was raised substantially in terms of increasing student numbers; at the same time teachers were subject to several re-organisations and waves of change in teaching methods.

It is impossible to say how much of rises in productivity come from greater efficiency, and how much from working harder. But the distinction is important. If new technology raises your daily output because, with the same expenditure of effort as before, you can get more letters written, contracts signed, or whatever, this is an unambiguous improvement in efficiency. If instead the new technology engenders a greater expenditure of effort from you than before, your employer benefits from your increased output performance, but the effect on you depends on whether the extra effort is welcome (given any change in wages).

To the extent that productivity rises come from work intensification, the concern is that such rises are comparatively short-term. Given that there are limitations to how hard people can work effectively, this mode of growth has a tendency towards satiation. A belief that productivity growth in the United States was being driven by work intensification led a leading management writer, Steven Roach of Morgan Stanley, to question four years ago the sustainability of US productivity growth.[4] Subsequent productivity performance has not yet served to confirm Roach's pessimism. High per capita growth rates for several years have been interpreted by a number of commentators as the eventual arrival of new technology's efficiency benefits, but this remains a controversial area. There are equally persuasive alternative candidates to explain high US growth, not least historically low energy prices and a facilitating monetary policy.

One reason why productivity rises can fail to materialise from effort intensification is if there is a simultaneous decrease in efficiency. Where the intensification is driven by ICT a commonly-reported concern is 'information-overload'. Since information is typically an 'experience good' – one whose value you cannot judge until you receive it – it is difficult for information receivers to determine the most efficient amounts to absorb. However the acceptance of information entails real costs. One of the problems of modern communication technologies is that receivers' costs are frequently substantial in relation to the transmission costs of the sender, especially when there are many receivers for each one sender. The technology permits, and encourages excessive information flows.

The need for policies on increasing work pressure

The most significant response to work intensification in Britain has been the growth of an occupational stress industry. Work stress has complex causes, but the connection with work intensification and work overload has been empirically well established, and is highly plausible. Individual responses include improved time management and stress management, and many responsible employers offer at least some training in these areas. The idea is partly that employees should learn to work harder without suffering deleterious effects. Individuals are also frequently urged to work 'smarter' rather than harder. In the pages of newspapers, there is a steady stream of advice about ways to reduce stress.

Individuals may also be able to respond to work intensification by choosing a job that most suits their effort preferences. Thus, if you do not want to work at the high pace required of, say, a city law firm, or a Silicon Valley consultancy, one can opt to work elsewhere for lower pay.

If individuals could always respond in such ways, there would be virtually no role for government to attempt to regulate work intensification. But the reality is a lot different. First, many individuals will have only a restricted choice over whom they can work for, given their past experiences. Most labour markets are more accurately characterised as monopsonies (many sellers, few buyers) than as in perfect competition. Second, in many jobs inputs of time and effort are easier to observe than their outputs in terms of job performance. In short, partial restrictions on job choices and the fear of sending the wrong signals may prevent individuals from opting for more desirable effort levels.

Firms also face constraints on the extent to which they could choose to provide jobs with optimal levels of work pressure. There may be insufficient incentives for firms to invest in health and safety measures, including restrictions on work pressure. This is because firms will not bear the full costs of health deterioration and/or industrial accidents. Rather, employees bear much of the cost, (in so far as any compensation is less than their health cost). Other employers also would bear some cost if they were to take on an individual with reduced productivity. In other words, for the same reason that firms may invest sub-optimally in training (Stevens, 1999), they may also require health-impairing excessive work loads, unless in some way regulated. There is, therefore, a collective role for regulation of work effort and work hours. The European Directive on Working Time presumably derives some justification from this fundamental argument. It is feared though that the Directive is having little impact on working hours because of widespread opt-outs, and insufficient policing of undue employee intimidation. Stricter enforcement of the Directive, and selective enlargement of its scope, should become a priority. Chapter 11 suggests a way of doing this.

There is also a more general case here for facilitating a collective voice at the workplace since, as the evidence suggests, the decline in the union voice is associated with a significantly larger rate of work intensification. It is no coincidence that near-neighbour countries like Belgium and Denmark, which have if anything increased the voice of unions in the 1990s, should have experienced much less work intensification than Britain. British unions will have to use what influence they have to try to gain for their members the choice to work at different effort rates according to their needs and preferences.

Looking to the future, indications of continued expansion of information and communications technologies and there being no sign of let-up in increasing levels of competitive pressures facing firms, it appears likely that jobs will continue to become more 'demanding' for an increasing proportion of Britain's workforce. The polarisation of life between the employed and the inactive, reflected in the opposites of time scarcity and time surplus, will continue. Yet if high-skilled and rewarding jobs are to continue to require high levels of work intensity, the need to generate high quality part-time or shorter-hours jobs becomes even more important.

We need to find ways of alleviating the negative consequences of workplace change, and a key element will be to permit both men and women to participate successfully at effort levels that suit their own work-life balance. It seems unlikely that individual-level solutions, valuable though they are, will solve the problem of work overload

I should like to thank my colleague Andrew Dickerson for his useful and creative comments on this paper.

Endnotes

1   An explanation of my sources for this chapter, plus many more details, is published in Green F (1999) *It's Been A Hard Day's Night: The Concentration And Intensification Of Work In Late 20th Century Britain* Discussion Paper 99/13, Department of Economics, University of Kent. A revised version was published in the British Journal of Industrial Relations in March 2001 (Green, 2001).

2   Source: the 1998 Workplace Employee Relations Survey, author's analysis.

3   I am indebted to Ewart Keep of Warwick University for this delightful term.

4   Roach (1996) also credits new technologies with raising actual work hours, saying they 'have created a portable assembly line...that allows white-collar workers to remain on-line in planes, trains, cars and home. So much for the liberating technologies of the Information Age.'

References

Braverman H (1974) *Labor and monopoly capital* New York, Monthly Review Press

Bresnahan T F (1999) 'Computerisation and Wage Dispersion: An Analytical Reinterpretation' *Economic Journal* 109: F390-F415

DfEE (1999) *Skills for the Information Age* Department for Education and Employment

DfEE (2000) *Skills for all: Research Report from the National Skills Task Force* Department for Education and Employment

Evans S, Ewing K and Nolan P (1992) 'Industrial-Relations and the British Economy in the 1990s-Thatcher Legacy' *Journal of Management Studies* 29 (5): 571-589

Felstead A, Green F and Mayhew K (1997) *Getting The Measure Of Training* Centre for Industrial Policy and Performance, University of Leeds

Gallie D and White M (1993) *Employee Commitment and the Skills Revolution* London, PSI Publishing

Green F (2001) 'It's Been A Hard Day's Night: The Concentration And Intensification Of Work In Late 20th Century Britain' *British Journal of Industrial Relations* (forthcoming, March)

Green F and Mcintosh S (1998) 'Union Power, Cost of Job Loss, and Workers' Effort' *Industrial & Labor Relations Review* 51 (3): 363-383

Green F and Mcintosh S (2000) *The Intensification of Work in Europe* Discussion Paper, Centre for Economic Performance, London School of Economics

Green F, Felstead A and Gallie D (2000) *Computers Are Even More Important Than You Think: An analysis of the changing skill-intensity of jobs* Discussion Paper 439, Centre for Economic Performance, London School of Economics

Green F, Ashton D, Burchell B, Davies B and Felstead A (2000) 'Are British Workers Getting More Skilled?' in Borghans L and de Grip A (eds) *The Over-Educated Worker? The Economics of Skill Utilisation* Edward Elgar

Oliver JM and Turton JR (1982) 'Is there a shortage of skilled labour?' *British Journal of Industrial Relations* (20): 195-200

O'Mahony M (1994) 'Can Britain Bridge The Productivity Gap?' *Long Range Planning* 27(2): 85-94

Office for National Statistics (1998) *Social Trends* 28 The Stationery Office

Reich R (1993) *American Competitiveness and American Brains* New York: Baruch College, City University of New York

Roach SS (1996) 'The hollow ring of the productivity revival' *Harvard Business Review* 74 (6): 81-86

Robinson P and Burkitt N (2000) 'The Challenge of Full Employment' IPPR Future of Work Seminar, 4 September

Stevens M (1999) 'Human Capital Theory and UK Vocational Training Policy' *Oxford Review of Economic Policy* 15 (1): 16-32

5. Wanting more from work? Aspirations and expectations of work

Laura Edwards and Nick Burkitt

One of the big questions for the future of employment policy is how far can we expect employees to demand and achieve improvements in their working lives, and in their own skills and human capital, in a mainly voluntaristic policy framework. Although there are areas where minimum standards will need to be raised or reinforced, the prospects for significant new rights outside the area of work-life balance and the equality agenda in the next few years would seem to be limited.

The ability or willingness of working people to seek and demand improvements for themselves is not only important in areas where they are encouraged to build on statutory minimum standards through voluntary agreement. Even gaining access to the new basic rights requires employees to know about and demand their statutory entitlements. Even if new enforcement mechanisms discussed in Chapter 11 are brought in, a new agency could only complement the existing system and help the more intractable cases.

This issue of raising employees' expectations so that they demand better working practices will be crucial to all the areas of policy described in the following chapters. The government's lifelong learning and skills agendas, for example, depend on people taking advantage of training and development opportunities offered in and out of work by their employer or the state. This will in turn depend on individuals wanting better work, seeing training and education as a way of achieving it, and knowing how to go about getting it.

In order to shed some light on this question, and to see which areas workers see as a particular priority, IPPR carried out some qualitative research among working people – asking them what they meant by good quality work, what were their aspirations and expectations of work, and how they expected to improve the quality of their working life (see Edwards and Burkitt, 2000, 2001). The research focused on low and middle paid workers, who are less likely to have access to some aspects of good 'quality of work', or be in a strong bargaining position.

Defining 'quality of work'

Job quality is difficult to define and definitions are inevitably subjective and multi-faceted. A number of authors writing on the subject have identified different elements of the characteristics and rewards of work, divided into 'intrinsic' and 'extrinsic' features (for example, Beatson, 2000). Intrinsic features include the nature of the work itself, how interesting it is, how much discretion and autonomy is allowed and the intensity of the work effort. Extrinsic features includes the level of pay and other benefits, job security, the opportunities for promotion and the practices available for work/ life balance such as leave or flexible hours. Since individuals rank the importance of these elements differently according to their preferences and circumstances, overall job quality is a subjective and personal concept which cannot be fully described, or measured objectively.

Not only do individuals value the various elements of a job differently, the importance of different elements of quality of work can change over time. Inglehart (1997) has argued that rich industrialised societies are moving from being characterised by materialist values, emphasising economic and physical security, towards 'post-materialist' values focusing on self-expression and quality of life. This would mean a shift in what motivates people to work, with income and security becoming less important over time, and the demand for interesting and meaningful work growing. This can also imply a greater focus on non-work activities and family life. Results from the British and European Social Attitudes surveys (Russell, 1998) suggest that more highly educated people place a higher value on intrinsic job characteristics. There is also evidence of a slight change over the 1990s, with the importance attached to income and opportunities for advancement falling slightly. On the other hand the importance attached to job security in Britain rose significantly between 1989 and 1997.

Employees' job satisfaction could be seen as a key measure of quality of work. There is a large body of literature and research on the topic, mainly within psychology but also in economics. David Guest looks in detail at this evidence in the following chapter, and at what it can tell us about what employees want. The key point is that the majority of employees say they are satisfied with their current job, although levels of satisfaction vary between different types of people and occupation.

Satisfaction does not always reflect objective measures of job quality, such as pay or degree of autonomy in the workplace. To a large extent it may depend on subjective criteria, such as meeting individual's needs and expectations. For example, although there is a weak positive relationship between pay and satisfaction, there is a stronger one with people's subjective views of their income relative to other comparable workers (Oswald and Clark, 1996). The fact that 'education appears to depress satisfaction with work', could be because higher levels of educational qualifications lead people to expect better quality and better rewarded work, which they do not always get.

Rose has identified 'skill discrepancies' as a key influence on job satisfaction: 'Lower personal skill predisposes people to higher job satisfaction – maybe their expectations are lower – while higher 'own-skill' levels make them more critical...Jobs moderately stretching personal skill boost job satisfaction, jobs poor in challenge stifle it.' He also identifies significant differences in reported satisfaction between occupations, which again do not show a simple relationship with status or pay (Rose, 1999, 2000). These are also linked to different 'rationales' for working, such as to get money for basics or for enjoyment or career development. Expectations of work, and therefore satisfaction with it, can be conditioned by the reasons that people work and the importance of their jobs to them.

People's attitudes to and expectations of work are also conditioned partly by their relationship with their employer. Both Mike Emmott and David Guest draw on the concept of 'psychological contract' as a way of understanding relationships at work in Chapters 6 and 7 (see also, Cully et al, 1999: Ch7). Employees' perception of this is a key predictor of overall job satisfaction.

Although people's expectations of work are vital in determining attitudes to their current jobs and what they want for the future, they are difficult to measure with quantitative methods. The introduction of a number of new policies and regulations affecting employment conditions could also mean that some people's attitudes have changed.

Focus group evidence

A total of twenty focus groups were carried out, each attended by between 6 and 8 people and lasting an hour and a half. The research was done in two stages. The first covered people earning under £10,000 per year or £5 per hour, with groups split into men and women and four different age groups from 18 to over 50 – eight in total. The second aimed to gauge how far the findings from this could be generalised up the income scale. Here, 12 groups were conducted, 6 with people earning between £10,000 and £16,000 per year (lower income group) and 6 with people earning £16,000 to £20,000 per year (middle income group).[1]

As a guide to where these employees stood in the labour market, seven per cent of men and 20 per cent of women in full time work earn less than £10,000 per year, and 29 per cent of men and 54 per cent of women earn less than £15,000 (ONS, 1999). The two income bands used for recruitment roughly cover the middle half of the women's income distribution, and the lower half of the men's. The lines were blurred though, by the presence of part-time workers, who on average earn less per hour, and people from different parts of the country with varied average pay rates.

The lower income groups included care workers, cleaners, painters and decorators, plumbers, childminders, hairdressers, factory workers, office administrators and couriers. The middle income groups included junior estate agents, sales people, call centre supervisors, data inputters, local authority officers, shop supervisors/lower managers and senior administrators.

The groups followed a flexible discussion guide, which broadly covered the following topics:

- Current experiences of work

- Expectations for the future

- Views on how 'quality of work' might be improved and whose responsibility it is to achieve it

- Awareness of and attitudes towards employee's rights in the workplace

- Three specific aspects of work were explored in more detail:
  - work-life balance,
  - participation in the workplace
  - learning and training

Key issues and concerns

There were as expected differences between the answers of the different age, sex and income groups, but some common themes came out of the discussions.

Most importantly, 'Quality of work' was not itself a top of mind issue for the majority of workers interviewed, regardless of income. While the importance of having an enjoyable working life and achieving job satisfaction is stressed, many countered this with a recognition that at work – perhaps more so than in other areas of life – people can't always get what they want. Work is an area of life where they expected to make trade-offs.

These low expectations stem partly from the reality of work that people are faced with. But there was also evidence of sticking with 'your lot' rather than challenging the status quo. This was very clearly the case among the lowest paid group. There was, not surprisingly, a clear correlation between people's earnings and expectations. Higher paid people expect to have more 'quality of work' factors in place, and as pay reflects bargaining power they are more likely to get them. The first round of research, with people earning under £5 per hour, suggested that although these workers wanted good employer relations, a good working environment and decent pay, they do not expect to get them. Typical quotes included:

> How enjoyable you think your working life will be is a bizarre question to ask, nobody has a working life they enjoy.
>
> *18-24 year old female, barmaid, Dunstable*

> Nobody I know feels appreciated or satisfied in their work
>> *24-40 year old male, factory worker, Liverpool*

> I'm just happy to have work, to have some security and to be earning a living
>> *40-50 year old male, airport worker, Hounslow*

Enhancing the quality of people's working lives therefore means encouraging them, particularly those on lower incomes, to expect to achieve it. Other common themes across the groups were:

- Awareness of employment rights, especially some of the newer ones such as parental leave, was patchy, although it was poorer among the lowest paid. Perhaps just as importantly, understanding of the details was limited, as was knowledge of how they might be enforced.

- There was more interest in and enthusiasm for addressing issues of work-life balance than other policy areas such as training or employee participation.

- Age and sex discrimination were commonly mentioned spontaneously across age groups and income brackets. This was an issue that a great many of the participants felt strongly about.

Employees' rights

There was agreement, at least among the better paid groups, that workers today enjoy much greater rights than those of previous decades. However, there is concern among some that rights do not apply equally to all; they are more accessible to some than others, with managers and more senior staff being treated more favourably.

> I think you're more protected these days...you can't be hired and fired at will, things like the minimum wage have been introduced.
>> *Female, 30-49, middle income bracket, Rochdale*

> The part time workers rights, thank God that's come in
>> *Female, 30-49, middle income bracket, Rochdale*

> They're starting this now aren't they, where men can get maternity leave...I think it's a good thing for the parents
>> *Female, 50-65, middle income bracket, Sheffield*

However, the Government is not explicitly or spontaneously mentioned as one that is committed to protecting workers. There is also concern among some that rights do not apply equally to all; they are more accessible to some than others, with managers and more senior staff being treated more favourably.

> I think it's double standards, it's a matter of 'if the cap fits, they're all right, we'll sort them out' but if you are a labourer or a manual worker then they'll treat you differently.
>
> *Male, 30-49, lower income bracket, Rochdale*

For some the increase in rights for workers has also run parallel to an increase in workloads and greater pressure on workers today. Older workers in particular often mentioned a trend towards people working longer hours and being expected to do more for their money.

> Workers have got more rights in a sense but they are also under more pressure.
>
> *Male, 50-65, lower income bracket, Coventry*

Respondents were first asked to spontaneously mention what rights they thought they were entitled to before being shown a list of current employment rights. The focus group participants were reasonably well informed regarding the range of rights available to them. Rights against unfair dismissal, entitlement to sick pay, holiday pay, breaks and maternity leave are often mentioned spontaneously. Awareness did seem to be greater among the higher earners than among the low paid.

However, there is less awareness of the new rights to unpaid parental leave and of the equal rights for part-time workers. There is also confusion around the detail of paternity rights for new fathers. It might be expected that rights which are new (Parental leave and the Part-time Regulations came into effect in December 1999 and July 2000 respectively) and apply only to certain sections of the workforce are less well know than others. On the other hand, their introduction generated media attention and debate, which might have been expected to raise their saliency in people's minds. There is as yet little evidence of the full extent of awareness of rights. The Department of Trade and Industry has commissioned surveys on awareness of new employment rights, among employers and employees, due to be published in 2001.[2]

Most of the rights available appeared to be in place for the majority of employees interviewed, and many felt able to negotiate time off when necessary. However, there were exceptions and a recognition that it is often easier to accept existing conditions rather than rock the boat and risk losing your job. The most frequently broken rights appeared to be those around working time. Many respondents have been asked to sign a 'get out' clause regarding the 48 hour working time directive; often it is included in initial contracts. Most accepted this as 'part of the job' however and in a number of cases it is seen as necessary in order to be able to do overtime and top up your income.

> We don't have breaks but, in saying that it's not quite a sweat shop…we can sit and talk…we just have a drink while we're working. I work for a company who tend to expect you to put in the hours; I'm supposed to do calls at night on top of my six days. They're fairly archaic, we don't even have lunch hours.
>
> *Female, 50-65, middle income bracket, Sheffield*

> My partner does longer than a 48 hour week, he does like 60 hours…but if he cut down to 48 he'd only get paid for 48. If he's used to 60 he's going to stick to it isn't he? And I'm used to him being out for 60 hours.
>
> *Female, 18-29, lower income bracket, Wallington*

More serious violations of workers rights appear to be around abuse of entitlements to sick pay and paid holiday. One worker described having to pay a £5 contribution a week towards sick pay. A number of part-time workers were unaware of their entitlement to some paid holiday and felt they would be unable to negotiate this with their employer.

> I don't think I could turn round to my boss and say I'm entitled to some paid holiday, he can be a bit difficult and I could do with the money so I don't want to upset that. I just do it and that's it.
>
> *Female, 30-49, lower income bracket, Southampton*

> There are loads of these agencies now and employers are using them because it's cheaper for them to pay temps to do the same job and there's no holiday pay, no sick pay.
>
> *Male, 30-49, lower income bracket, Rochdale*

> It's all very well knowing your rights but if you push the issue too much you find yourself out of a job
>
> *Male, lower income bracket, 50-65 years old, Wallington*

This raises the question of how employees can go about enforcing their rights, once they are aware that they have been breached. There was little knowledge of how one might go about doing so.

Discrimination

Both age and sex discrimination were commonly mentioned spontaneously as issues affecting people's working lives and the opportunities that are open to them. The de-valuing and under-valuing of the skills and experience of older workers is a common complaint among those in the older age group (50-65) and was also recognised as an issue by those in the middle age group (30-49).

Age discrimination

Age was seen as a barrier to getting jobs – particularly getting to the interview stage – and also a factor that can play a part in losing a job. The experience and reliability of older workers was often felt to be ignored. A few employers were seen to be better at this, such as B&Q and Sainsbury's.

> Experience counts for nothing half the time. They just want whizz kids.
>
> *Male, 50-65, lower income bracket, Coventry*

> I felt discriminated against because of my age when I was made redundant because they took on someone straight out of college to replace me, without any experience at all.
>
> *Male, 50-65, middle income bracket, Wallington*

Sex discrimination

Sex discrimination was mentioned by women in all age groups and across the income brackets. Men in the younger age group (18-29) were also conscious that their female counterparts can be discriminated against when, for example, they become pregnant. Sex discrimination plays itself out in a number of different ways in the workplace, the most commonly described was women being asked about family commitments at job interviews and being questioned about their ability to juggle work and home responsibilities; something they felt men do not have to contend with.

> I felt like I was being victimised for being a young mum...you feel like you have to go into the interview like you are a working girl...I think they questioned my commitment and thought I'd abandon the job as soon as there was a problem with the children.
>
> *Female, 30-49, lower income bracket, Southampton*

It's discriminating, you get asked everything else and you think you've done ok and then it's like, 'Have you got a child? What are you going to do with them in school holidays?' and you just feel stupid, and you think, well, what's it to you? They shouldn't really ask you...it shouldn't be an issue whether you've got children or not.

Female, 18-29, lower income bracket, Wallington

Differentials in pay were also mentioned, particularly by women in the older age groups. More generally there was a sense among some that women have to try harder to prove themselves and get what they deserve in the workplace.

When I compare with the chaps I work with, what they're earning and what I'm earning, there is a significant difference, not just a little bit. We're doing very similar jobs and I've also been the longest with the company.

Female, 50-65, middle income bracket, Sheffield

The job I do for social services is dominated by women and because we're not full-time we're treated like peripheral workers...that's what we're actually called.

Female, 30-49, lower income bracket, Southampton

Work-life balance

Work-life balance issues received a more positive response than ideas around participation and training for improving quality of work. When asked, the majority of respondents, particularly men, were quick to recognise that their own work-life balance is not ideal and that they would prefer to have more time to spend with their family and friends outside of work.

I think there's more important things in life than just work, you've got to have free time, you've got to have a social life and you've got to be happy in what you do.

Female, 18-29, middle income bracket, Coventry

I think we are working a lot more now than we ever have done...I work harder now for what I get out of it than I used to.

Male, 50-65, lower income bracket, Coventry

I find it awful because we are on 24 hour cover...when everybody is coming home, you're going out to work so you have missed a part of your life

Male, 30-49, lower income bracket, Rochdale

There was a widespread desire to improve their work-life balance but at the same time a feeling that this is unachievable. Particularly for those in the middle income bracket there was an awareness of the need sometimes to prove yourself at work by staying late or working overtime. For lower earners especially, trading pay for free time or flexibility was seen as unfeasible.

There was a clear gender divide in responses to flexible ways of working. Women in all age groups are much more likely to experiment with flexible ways of working, in particular part-time working, and recognise that they may want to alter their working hours at different life stages. The majority of the men interviewed also saw flexible ways of working as more likely options for women. Men could see the value in spending more time with families and less time at work but few wanted to do it themselves or believed it was personally feasible. Men were more likely to feel that on a practical level it 'just wouldn't work' and were less likely than women to feel that they could make the trade off between more free time and less pay. For many of the men, the link between work and family was articulated in terms of more work equaling more money to support your family.

You've got no choice have you? To have that quality time you have to work and put the hours in, otherwise you can't afford the things your family wants.

Male, 30-49, Lower income bracket, Rochdale

There might be a lot of people who can do that but there will be an awful lot of people who can't take a drop in what they are getting now because they are struggling to live on what they have got now.

Male, 50-65, lower income bracket, Coventry

Many participants also raised issues of practicality. The most fundamental of these is that some jobs simply do not lend themselves to flexible models of working. Jobs that are more likely to lend themselves to flexible ways of working are seen to be those which involve lots people doing either the same or similar jobs or jobs in larger companies where employees would be able to cover each other. The other key feasibility issue was being in a position to negotiate a change in working hours with your employer. For some, particularly men and those on lower incomes this ability to negotiate did not seem realistic.

The majority of the group participants welcomed the extended rights to parental leave for those with young children. Respondents were also asked whether they would be willing to pay for this leave. There was clear agreement that if parental leave is not paid for then the majority of people are unlikely to take full advantage of it. Men in particular were unlikely to trade lost wages for more time with their families and those on low wages are also unlikely to be able to afford to do so.

> If you are having a child you can't afford to take it because you want the money, you're working to bring the money in to support the child.
> *Male, 30-49, lower income bracket, Rochdale*

However, the response was divided as to whether or not this leave should be paid and there was evidence of a potential backlash towards such 'family-friendly' policies among certain groups. The backlash was particularly evident amongst the youngest and the oldest age groups (18-29 and 50–65) and is more prevalent among men than women. Within these age groups few are willing to pay more in taxes to fund paid parental leave and a number believe paid leave would be abused and could potentially harm small businesses.

Support for paid parental leave was however evident among women in the 30-49 age bracket and men in the middle income bracket aged 30-49. Those in favour of such a policy recognise it is an important incentive that would encourage more parents to take it. Women are particularly conscious of the need for parental leave to be paid in order to encourage men, and not just women, to use it. Some suggest partially paid parental leave as a compromise.

> Maternity leave is subsidised by the government anyway so why can't paternity leave be the same?
> *Male, 30-49, middle income bracket, Southampton*

Participation

Being listened to, having a say and feeling like you have somewhere to voice concerns and complaints in the workplace was important to the majority of employees interviewed. However, participation issues tended not to be top of employees' minds when thinking about quality of work.

Responses in the focus groups suggest that informal mechanisms are valued more by employees as they are less confrontational and fit in with the concept of the workplace as a place of social interaction where there is the same give and take as in other areas of life. In contrast, formal mechanisms to have your say in the workplace can be seen as old-fashioned and associated with trade unions and adversarial work relations.

There was evidence that employers themselves are becoming more aware of the need to inform and consult their employees. Those in the middle income bracket frequently described having regular staff meetings, being kept informed through company newsletters, having access to information on the company intranet and being consulted formally regarding changes. In the lower income bracket staff meetings were also fairly common and many describe feeling able to informally approach their employer and line managers with problems and comments.

> The company I work for does seem to be trying to change the old culture and bring in something new...they'll lose their competitive edge if they don't modernise their thinking and allow their shop floor people to participate more.
>
> *Male, 50-65, lower income bracket, Coventry*

However, this picture of employers willing to listen is not true across the board. There was some evidence that on big decisions – for example restructuring the working day – employees can easily be excluded from decisions. For a number of respondents the desire was for a more open, two-way dialogue between employers and employees where they could move away from feeling that they were 'the last to know' about decisions made in the workplace.

> You need to feel like a person and not just a number. It's true in a lot of jobs that you just end up conforming and you do what they tell you to do; you very rarely get asked your opinion.
>
> *Female, 18-29, lower income bracket, Wallington*

> They've completely changed our shifts round at the moment and haven't even told anyone about it yet, I just heard it on the grapevine and confronted someone about it. There was no consultation...they now expect us to work four out of five weekends
>
> *Female, 24-40, Cardiff*

Establishing more formal mechanisms for employees to have a say in decision-making, such as works councils, was welcomed by some as a move in the right direction. Furthermore, regular mechanisms for communication were seen as a positive step – if not always realistic.

However, questions are raised regarding whether such mechanisms really harness power for workers. Some with experience of formal consultations, for example regarding company take-overs or restructuring, suggest that their employer was just paying lip service to the process. Although the process itself is seen as important there was a level of cynicism as to employers' motives for consulting.

Training

There is a general recognition that further training and qualifications can lead to more pay and better job prospects but many feel it is too late to 'start again'. Those most open to pursuing further qualifications are the younger respondents in the middle income bracket who tend to be more confident that a qualification will help them to progress. For others, there was often a desire to do some further training but this can be combined with a lack of clarity on what course would be best, a fear of feeling out of place, a concern that costs are too high and scepticism that it might not pay off.

> The thing is, as you get older, you get in a rut, you should have done it when you left school at 17...but a lot of people don't realise until they are older and they think, well hang on, I'm not going anywhere.
>
> *Female, 18-29, lower income bracket, Wallington*

> Sometimes I get a bit bored because I think, oh, you know, I've got a brain and I'm not using it at all. I'm thinking about going to night classes at college but the money is a problem.
>
> *Female, 18-29, lower income bracket, Wallington*

> I went to college for this qualification and I was supposed to get this perfect job now. I went to two really good interviews and I didn't get either of them for completely different reasons. It really affected me, I had found a childminder for my children and I was ready to give it all up. I took the course and struggled doing it but it just hasn't turned out the way that I'd expected.
>
> *Female, 30-49, lower income bracket, Southampton*

A training gap was identified by some of those in the younger age bracket (18-30 year olds) who are beginning to come up against a pay barrier as they try to progress at work. In this age group, particularly among those on middle incomes, there was a readiness to gain further qualifications but at the same time a feeling that if you haven't got a degree then your chances of moving up the pay scale are fairly limited. On the other hand for some in the younger age groups, particularly those on lower incomes, more likely opportunities for furthering their career were making it on your own' by running your own business and becoming your own boss. Some are content to stick with what they know, even in the youngest age bracket.

When I was at school I used to think, 'oh yeah, I'm going to be...', I don't know, oh loads of things I wanted to be but it never quite happened, I wasn't clever enough so I just sort of gave up on those ideas. But it doesn't bother me because all my mates are the same and I've got money in my pocket and I'm having a good enough life.

Female, 18-29, lower income bracket, Wallington

Policy implications

This chapter details the themes and responses that emerged within a series of focus group discussions. As a qualitative research study the findings are based on interpretation and analysis of responses. It cannot tell how views are distributed amongst the population. That is what the quantitative evidence in the following chapter aims to do. However it does provide other opportunities to understand public thinking. Qualitative research is useful for highlighting the range of attitudes and level of interest regarding a particular issue and also for respondents to raise issues of concern that may not be picked up on in a quantitative study.

The findings of the focus groups highlight a number of issues and challenges for a Government that is committed to enhancing quality and not just quantity of work:

- There is a need for more information to help people right across the workforce understand what are often complex rules around employment rights. Full implementation of new and existing rights will involve publicising them more.

- There is enthusiasm for tackling work-life balance issues, and more so than for action in the area of training or workforce participation. However, the strategy of promoting the benefits of new arrangements to all workers and employers, not just mothers and big firms, still has a long way to go. It is also important to recognise that 'quality of work' is a much more feasible option for those earning more money.

- 'Quality of work' is itself not the most accessible language to frame policy. The focus groups suggest a very limited understanding of what has already been done and what is planned under the 'Fairness at Work' and Work-life balance agendas. 'Job satisfaction', giving people 'quality time' and 'working to live rather than living to work' are more everyday ways of expressing the same ideas.

- Many of the focus group participants spontaneously mentioned discrimination on the grounds of sex and gender. Sex and disability discrimination laws have of course been in effect for many years, but were not seen as fully effective or accessible as remedies. The new Code of Practice on Age Diversity had not made any impact that these groups were aware of.

- A strategy of improvements over and above minimum standards of decency that is based on voluntaristic mechanisms will require a cultural shift. This means challenging a culture of low expectations at work. But it is difficult to draw a line between low expectations or cynicism and simple realism. The fact that people have different levels of bargaining power in the labour market, and that some are in an unacceptably weak situation, is the reason that the state intervenes in the employment relationship.

Endnotes

1   For full details of methodology, see Edwards and Burkitt (2001)

2   Studies by Kingston Business School and Institute for Employment Studies, forthcoming 2001.

References

Beatson M (2000) 'Job "quality" and forms of employment: concepts and the UK statistical evidence' Paper for ILO seminar on Measurement of the quality of employment May 2000.

Cully M, Woodland S, O'Reilly A and Dix G (1999) *Britain at Work as depicted by the 1998 Workplace Employee Relations Survey* London: Routledge

Edwards L and Burkitt N (2001) *Wanting more from Work? Aspirations and expectations of people in low and middle paid jobs* DfEE Research Brief RBX 6-01

Edwards L and Burkitt N (2000) *The Future of Work: findings of a series of focus groups with people in low paid jobs* IPPR

Ingelhart R (1997) *Modernisation and post modernisation: Cultural, Economic and Political Change in 43 Societies* Princeton University Press

Office for National Statistics (1999) *New Earnings Survey* 1999

Oswald A and Clark A (1996) 'Satisfaction and Comparison Income' *Journal of Public Economics* 61, 359-381

Rose M (2000) *Work Centrality, Work Careers, and Household: Let's Ask for Numbers* Report to ESRC Future of Work programme, September 2000

Rose M (1999) *Explaining and forecasting job satisfaction: the contribution of occupational profiling* Working Paper 3, ESRC Future of Work programme, Leeds University Business School/Swindon

Russell H (1998) 'The Rewards of Work' in *British Social Attitudes, the 15th Report*

6. We've never had it so good? An analysis of what workers want from work

David Guest

Can we know what workers want?

There is a long and unhelpful record of research by organisational psychologists asking people what they want from work. Usually, workers have not thought seriously about this or cannot articulate their wants very clearly. Responses depend partly upon how the question is asked and what choices are offered. However, near the top of the list we invariably find a desire for interesting work, congenial colleagues, a supportive boss, a degree of job security and reasonable pay.

One popular approach has been to ask the lottery question. If you won enough money never to need to work again, what would you do? In most countries the great majority say they would continue to work. In a comparative survey in the 1980s, 69 per cent of British workers (the lowest in any of the seven countries covered) said they would continue to work. In a 1996 survey, this figure had fallen to 60 per cent. The information from Camelot suggests that over 50 per cent of major lottery winners continue to do some sort of work, although often a change of employment including a move to self-employment takes place. What all this implies is that work remains a central life interest for most workers and they do not work solely for money.

A recent survey by Roffey Park (Glynn, 2000), to which 1,681 young people still at school responded, indicated that the three top priorities for work were that it should be interesting, pay well and leave time for outside interests. The survey also revealed limited knowledge about the realities of working life. In a recent survey of the state of the employment relationship (Guest and Conway, 2000), individuals were asked to identify the single change at work that would most improve their working life in the next year. 29 per cent cited more pay and benefits, 11 per cent a reduced workload and/or shorter hours and 9 per cent mentioned promotion/advancement. This is very much a conventional wish list, although the concern for workload and hours may indicate a more contemporary issue.

Rather than dealing with abstractions and ideal circumstances, analysis of workers aspirations and priorities is probably best grounded in their experience and located in an organisational and national policy context.

Current policy and practice at work: Why we've never had it so good

If we start from current UK employment policy and practice, we can make a strong case that at the start of the new millennium, workers are better off than ever in many and probably most respects. We now have legislation covering many of the areas that affect the quality of working life. These include:

- equal opportunities

- safety at work

- working hours

- minimum wage

- union recognition

- family-friendly practices

- protection of personal information

- Works Councils in large multinational organisations

In addition, we have recent legislation on human rights with its potential to affect working lives and forthcoming legislation limiting discrimination at work including age discrimination. Beyond legislation we have

- a high degree of working hours flexibility to facilitate work-life balance

- fewer people working in machine-paced jobs

- strong encouragement and public debate about a raft of family-friendly practices as well as government-sponsored company-based initiatives

- strong encouragement of partnership at work

- rising real wages for a majority of workers

- a relatively tight labour market with low levels of job insecurity

- the New Deals to help those on the margins of work to enter employment

- claimant unemployment down to about one million, its lowest level for over 20 years

- an historically low level of strikes and industrial conflict

In short, the Labour government, whether by accident or design, sometimes with enthusiasm and sometimes dragging its feet, appears to have done a great deal to improve work. As a result, the objective conditions in which people experience work are arguably better than ever before for more people than ever before. On this basis, we would expect to find most people reporting high levels of job satisfaction and satisfaction with the quality of working life. And we would expect that levels of job satisfaction have been rising.

The evidence on job satisfaction and life satisfaction

Organisational psychologists have published well over 3000 papers on job satisfaction and the subject has now begun to interest economists such as Andrew Oswald. A review of national studies of job satisfaction (Guest and Conway, 1999) shows those most British workers are satisfied although relatively few are very satisfied. Differences in wording make direct comparisons difficult and there is some dispute about the value of asking a general question on overall job satisfaction (Rose, 2000, Wanous, Reichers and Hudy, 1997); but Table 6.1 gives an indication of responses from representative national surveys.

Table 6.1

Survey	Question	Responses										
CIPD 1998 (n = 1000)	How satisfied are you with your work?	*totally dissatisfied*					*%*					*totally satisfied*
		1	*2*	*3*	*4*	*5*	*6*	*7*	*8*	*9*	*10*	
		2	1	3	4	12	13	18	26	10	9	
GHS 1990s (n = 5000)	All things considered, how satisfied or dissatisfied are you with your present job overall?	*not satisfied at all*				*%*						*completely satisfied*
			1	*2*	*3*	*4*	*5*	*6*	*7*			
			2	3	6	9	21	42	18			
BSA 1997 (n = 623)	How satisfied are you in your job?	*not satisfied at all*				*%*						*completely satisfied*
			1	*2*	*3*	*4*	*5*	*6*	*7*			
			1	2	8	9	44	22	13			
EURB 1996 (n = 1064)	How satisfied (or dissatisfied) are you in your job?	*very dissatisfied*		*a little dissatisfied*			*moderately satisfied*			*very satisfied*		
		10		9			49			38		

Source: Annual survey of the Chartered Institute of Personnel and Development (CIPD), the General Household Survey (GHQ) which contains a panel survey, the British Social Attitudes (BHS) survey and Eurobarometer (EURB)

Despite some variations in the degree of satisfaction, about 80 per cent say they are satisfied with their work. Far fewer claim to be very satisfied with their jobs While there is often quite a high zone of indifference, it is rare to find more than 25 per cent admitting that they are dissatisfied with their jobs.

Oswald (Oswald and Gardner, 2001) has analysed trends in job satisfaction in the UK using the British Household Panel Survey. This reveals a slow decline in job satisfaction from an average on a 7-point scale of 5.47 in 1991 to 5.32 in 1998, although this hides an upward trend in 1997 and 1998. The decline, from a higher starting point, has been steeper among women than men, though by the end of the decade, women still remain significantly more satisfied with their jobs than men. Similarly, the decline has been more pronounced in the public than in the private sector, again from a higher starting point and again with public sector employees remaining on average more satisfied. Of course we need to be careful in making comparisons across large sectors since this hides intra-sector differences. For example, Oswald and Gardner report particularly high levels of job satisfaction among those working in not-for-profit organisations and Guest and Conway (2000) found that workers in central government and its agencies were less satisfied than those in health and local government. Leaving aside these differences, the key point from the time-series data are that despite objective indicators of improvements affecting some core aspects of work, job satisfaction has tended to decline. Since Blanchflower and Oswald have presented evidence of a modest decline in job satisfaction in the USA during a period of increasing affluence (Blanchflower and Oswald, 1999), there is a good indication that subjective job satisfaction is poorly associated, if at all, with objective economic conditions.

Further support for this assertion comes from comparative data. In most comparative surveys, the UK does not fare well, with the UK workforce either in the middle or below in a rank order of job satisfaction among industrial countries. This is the case even when comparisons are made with some of the poorer nations. A more realistic comparison can probably be made with other EU countries. The 1996 Eurobarometer data shows the UK ranked 8th out of 16 EU countries (East and West Germany were treated separately but are very similar with East Germans the slightly more satisfied). Ireland tops the list on job satisfaction, although on certain objective indicators we might not expect it to do so.

We can look beyond job satisfaction to measures of well-being and life satisfaction to provide some kind of check on these counter-intuitive trends. Oswald and Gardner report the results of time-series data using the General Health Questionnaire (GHQ) as part of the British Household Panel Survey between 1991 and 1998. The GHQ is an initial indicator of mental health and well-being. The panel data show a decline in well-being between 1991 and 1995 after which it stabilises but does not improve.

If we are interested in any impact of government policy initiatives and economic trends since the change of government in 1997, then we really need data that extend beyond 1998. The annual CIPD surveys, although based on relatively modest sample sizes, can give an indication of the more recent trends in job satisfaction. The figures in the Table below indicate that the decline in job – or in this case, work – satisfaction may have been halted. There is also some indication of rising satisfaction with certain aspects of life outside work and most notably satisfaction with life as a whole. Where direct comparisons were possible between 1998 and 1999, workers in traditional blue- collar jobs were the most likely to show increased overall life satisfaction.

The surveys also tell us about other aspects of working life. The most recent CIPD survey, for 2000, shows that among those in industry, 71 per cent believe they have a satisfactory balance between work and life outside work (see Table 6.2). Those who have the poorer balance are, predictably, those working longer hours but also women rather than men, those with dependent children and trade union members. They are also likely to be part of management and to have higher earnings, reflecting the fact that those working long hours are often in management grades. More worryingly, there is some evidence that use of family friendly practices, while it may possibly help to ameliorate the imbalance, does not result in a satisfactory balance between work and life outside work.

Table 6.2: CIPD Annual Surveys of The State of the Employment Relationship

	1998	1999	2000
Satisfaction with			
Your life as a whole	7.37	7.52	7.69
Your family and friends	8.39	8.55	8.69
Your health	7.87	7.90	8.16
Your work	6.93	6.87	6.99
Your finances	6.34	6.51	6.33
Your employer			6.68
Balance between work and life outside work			6.84

The responses show the average score across the sample. Responses are based on a 10 point scale from totally dissatisfied (1) to totally satisfied (10). The 1998 sample is based on a random sample of 1000 workers. The 1999 sample is based on 493 of the 1998 sample who were followed up a year later and who were in the same job. The 2000 sample is based on 500 private sector workers. Public sector workers are, on average, more positive on each item.

The same survey shows that in 2000, 57 per cent of private sector workers claim to work more than their contracted hours in a typical week, including 14 per cent working over 48 hours a week. When asked why they work beyond their contracted hours, 55 per cent say they do so out of personal choice, 17 per cent because they are forced to by circumstances at work and 27 per cent say it is a bit of both.

These results should be seen in the context of evidence that work remains an important part of most people's lives. Asked whether they were more committed to work or life outside work, 19 per cent of private sector workers cited work, 27 per cent life outside work but 54 per cent said they were equally committed to both. This indicates that if we are to understand the well-being and life satisfaction of people, then their experience of work is likely to be a crucial factor.

In summary, while evidence from a range of policy initiatives and from objective indicators such as real wage rises and falling unemployment suggest that there should be an overall improvement in job satisfaction, the survey evidence challenges this assumption. Indeed, there is sufficient evidence from the surveys to show that there is no clear association between economic conditions and the objective characteristics of work and employees' subjective experiences of job satisfaction and well-being. This confirms what social scientists have known for a long time, namely that to understand work satisfaction and its link to life satisfaction and general well-being, we need analytic frameworks that take more fully into account the expectations and experiences associated with work.

What determines work satisfaction?

While the question of the level of job satisfaction is of interest in itself, from a policy perspective it is possibly more important to explain variations in job satisfaction.

There are some consistent individual background factors that help to identify the more or less satisfied workers. Some of the recent UK evidence, drawn from the annual CIPD surveys and the Workplace Employee Relations Survey is summarised in Table 6.3.

Table 6.3 Individual factors explaining satisfaction and dissatisfaction

		CIPD Surveys	WERS
$N =$		2000	28500
Tenure		–0.052*	–0.091***
Permanent contract		0.042	0.040***
Hours worked		0.003	–0.060***
Trade union member		–0.105***	–0.121***
Male		0.104***	–0.092***
Education		–0.063*	–0.034***
Age		0.058*	0.090***
Blue-collar worker		–0.109***	–0.141***
White-collar worker		–0.058*	–0.102***
Service and sales worker		0.042	0.013
Income		0.088**	0.079***

A positive sign indicates an association with satisfaction. The table shows beta weights derived from regression analysis. Asterisks indicate levels of statistical significance ranging from * ($p<0.05$) and ** ($p<0.01$) to *** ($p<0.001$).

There is a consistent pattern in the results across the surveys shown here which is largely confirmed by Oswald and Gardner's data using the British Household Panel Survey. The most satisfied workers are likely to be older, female, in management or professional jobs as opposed to traditional white-collar or blue-collar jobs, with a higher income. In contrast, satisfaction is lower among those with higher educational qualifications, with longer tenure and among trade union members. Although they are not shown here, organisational characteristics can also make a difference and satisfaction is higher in the public sector in general and in smaller organisations and establishments. Although analysis of individual characteristics is useful, we need to go a step further to identify the policies and practices that make a difference. One research framework increasingly used to analyse workers concerns and link them to corporate policy and practice is based on the concept of the psychological contract.

The *psychological contract* can be defined as 'The perceptions of both parties to the employment relationship, organisation and individual, of the reciprocal promises and obligations implied in the relationship'. It has come to the fore on the basis of an assumption that the traditional employment relationship, whether it is based on 'a fair day's work for a fair day's pay' or 'loyalty in return for a career' has broken down but not been replaced by any clear alternative. It is further argued that rapid change at work inevitably leads to contract violations by both sides with consequent reductions in commitment among employees and willingness to invest in employees among organisations. In practice, these underlying assumptions can be challenged. Nevertheless, the concept provides a useful framework for analysing policy issues in the context of the individualisation of the employment relationship and in helping to explain variations in job satisfaction.

At the heart of the psychological contract, workers will believe that the organisation has certain obligations to them and will have made a number of promises and commitments. The state of the psychological contract can be operationalised, from a worker's perspective, in terms of the extent to which the organisation has delivered its promises and commitments, the fairness with which they are treated and the level of trust in management to look after their interests and to keep their promises in the future. For example, the 2000 CIPD survey shows that among those working in private industry, 71 per cent believe their employer made a promise 'to provide fair pay for the work you do' and in 52 per cent of cases, workers said the promise had been fully kept. Only 3 per cent said it had not been kept at all, the remainder saying it had been partly kept. 42 per cent said their organisation had promised to provide interesting work and 49 per cent had kept the promise in full.

Building on fairness of treatment, 69 per cent of those in the private sector believe they are 'definitely' or 'probably' fairly rewarded for the amount of effort they put into their job while just over 30 per cent do not. 35 per cent trust their organisation 'a lot' and 39 per cent 'somewhat' to keep its promises and commitments to them. Taken as a whole, these results indicate that the psychological contract of a majority of workers appears to be in reasonably good shape; but for a sizeable minority this is not the case.

One of the reasons why the psychological contract is useful is that it serves as a form of cognitive appraisal by workers of management policy and practice. In other words, management may institute a policy. What matters, in terms of workers' reactions, is how they appraise it. Do they believe it is there to help or to exploit workers? Is it serious or, as cynical workers may suspect, a bit of fashionable window-dressing that can be ignored because it is likely soon to be dropped or superseded? Does it fit with their experiences and expectations of what is reasonable and of what the organisations should do? The assessment of the state of the psychological contract provides us with an opportunity to explore how workers appraise policy and practice and the impact this has on job satisfaction and other work-related attitudes and behaviour.

An analysis of the antecedents and consequences of the psychological contract are shown in Figure 6.1, which is based on the 1998 CIPD survey. The figure shows the background and policy factors significantly associated with a positive psychological contract and the links between the psychological contract and a range of outcomes including job satisfaction and life satisfaction. The results also indicate that the psychological contract effectively mediates the relationship between context, policy and practice and employee outcomes.

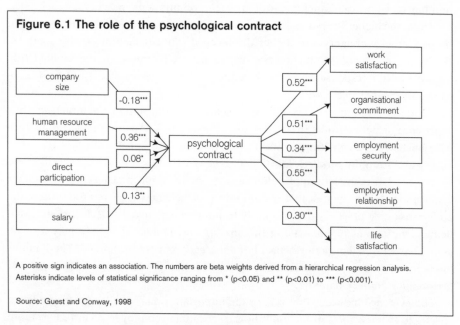

Figure 6.1 The role of the psychological contract

A positive sign indicates an association. The numbers are beta weights derived from a hierarchical regression analysis. Asterisks indicate levels of statistical significance ranging from * ($p<0.05$) and ** ($p<0.01$) to *** ($p<0.001$).

Source: Guest and Conway, 1998

The analysis confirms that human resource practices and scope for participation and autonomy in the job have an important impact on the state of the psychological contract and hence on satisfaction. Essentially, the more that workers report that they experience a set of progressive human resource practices, the more positive they are about the psychological contract and the more satisfied they are with their work and with life as a whole. Importantly, this implies some spillover effect from work to the rest of life.

While the analysis above highlights the mediating role of the psychological contract and the process of appraisal implied by it, human resource management and a climate of involvement also have a direct association with job satisfaction in analysis of the Workplace Employee Relations Survey. As well as demonstrating the association between greater use of human resource management and aspects of consultation and job satisfaction and commitment, the results also confirm the negative association with size of establishment and organisation and show a negative association between trade union density and job satisfaction/commitment.

The role of human resource management

Human resource policy and practice appears to have an association with a positive state of the psychological contract and both indirectly through this and directly, with job satisfaction and other positive attitudes. The responses are based on a count of the number of what are sometimes called 'high commitment' practices. Essentially, therefore, the higher the number of practices in place, as reported either by workers or by personnel managers, the higher the level of job satisfaction among workers. Workers' accounts of the practices they experience are monitored in the annual CIPD surveys and the responses are fairly consistent over the years. The 1998 figures are shown overleaf (Table 6.4).

Workers give surprisingly positive accounts of the number of practices they experience or believe to be in place in their organisation. Analyses of accounts from personnel managers are less positive. Figures from the Workplace Employee Relations Survey and from the Birkbeck ESRC Future of Work study (Guest *et al*, 2000 a and b) suggest that consistent application of these policies and practices may be rather lower. Indeed, they suggest that organisations are generally reluctant to invest in the human resource practices that are likely to improve employee satisfaction and well-being. One argument for making this investment, namely that they may also be associated with higher performance, has apparently not yet hit home. Mike Emmott looks in more detail at the link between good HR practices and organisational performance in the Chapter 7.

The evidence indicates that one of the important policy challenges facing those seeking to increase job satisfaction is how to encourage employers to introduce more human resource practices. Legislation can help, as reflected by the responses on equal opportunity and the government as an employer can help to set a good

Table 6.4 Workers' experience of human resource management n=1000

	% responses		
	Yes	No	Don't know
Your organisation actively carries out equal opportunities practices in the workplace	86	10	4
Your employer provides you with sufficient opportunities for updating your skills through training and development	80	20	1
Your organisation keeps you well informed about business issues and about how well it is doing	77	22	1
When new positions come up in management, your company normally tries to fill them with people from inside the organisation rather than recruit them from outside	57	37	7
You receive formal performance appraisals	54	44	1
Your organisation tries to get employee more involved in workplace decision-making using things like self-directed work teams, total quality management, quality circles and involvement programmes	53	43	3
There is a serious attempt to make the jobs of people like you as interesting and varied as possible	51	45	4
Your organisation has a stated policy of deliberately avoiding compulsory redundancies and lay-offs	36	36	28
Your organisation has established facilities to help employees deal with non-work responsibilities. These are sometimes termed family-friendly policies, such as on-site child-care facilities, counselling for non-work problems, financial planning and legal services	34	62	4
Your pay is related to your performance in some way	30	70	0

Source: Guest and Conway (1998)

example. Pressure can also come from other sources. The evidence from some surveys indicates that more of the progressive human resource practices will be in place where there is a professional personnel department and a trade union presence.

Autonomy and partnership at work

The second policy issue emerging from surveys using the psychological contract framework concerns the importance of employee autonomy, involvement and consultation at work. The surveys cited earlier indicate that workers place a high value on interesting work and on some control over what they do and how they do it. At the same time they suggest that scope for local autonomy is still heavily restricted for some workers. The WERS survey, which covered some 28000 workers, provides evidence on this (Table 6.5).

Table 6.5 Perceptions of autonomy and consultation (WERS, 1998)

		% responses		
		Public sector	Private sector	Total
In general, how much influence do you have about th the range of tasks you do in your job?	a lot	23	26	25
	some	42	38	39
	a little	19	18	18
	none	15	18	17
In general, how much influence do you have about th the pace at which you work?	a lot	30	35	34
	some	39	35	37
	a little	17	16	16
	none	13	14	14
In general, how much influence do you have about how you do your work?	a lot	44	49	47
	some	41	33	36
	a little	11	12	11
	none	4	6	6
How often are you and others working here asked by managers for your views on changes to work practices?	frequently	19	17	17
	sometimes	48	42	44
	hardly ever	15	15	15
	never	19	27	24

Source: Cully et al (1999)

While quite a high proportion of workers report 'some' influence, less than a third report a lot of influence. Not surprisingly those in managerial and professional jobs report higher levels of influence. The survey also reported low levels of collective bargaining and consultation in a majority of workplaces. In short, levels of autonomy and consultation are relatively low and an increase is likely to be associated with increased job satisfaction.

One possible route to enhanced autonomy is through partnership which has been strongly endorsed by the government and the TUC. Research among members of the Involvement and Participation Association (IPA), who might be expected to be at the leading edge of good practice on partnership, reveals that managers and workers' representatives rate the scope for direct participation in day-to-day work as a key factor in successful partnership. However it also confirms that the scope for such participation is low. Evidence of the benefits of direct participation also emerge in the detailed analyses undertaken by Keith Sisson and others for the EU (EPOC Research Group, 1997). In this respect the UK lags behind Europe.

Nevertheless, however strong the case for partnership may be on other grounds, we should be cautious about expecting it to have a direct link to job satisfaction. Partnership deals can create a context and unions can lay a valuable part in ensuring that momentum is maintained. The evidence suggests, though, that such deals rarely lead on to increased autonomy for the majority of workers. The policy challenge is how to move build on partnership deals to ensure that the basis for high trust that such deals can engender leads to increased autonomy on the shop or office floor with consequent improvements in job satisfaction.

Concern for the low levels of worker autonomy is linked to a third policy issue. Studies of the psychological contract support other surveys in highlighting concerns about the intensity and duration of work and a desire for a balance between work and life outside work. Workload is one of the issues on which workers are most likely to believe that the organisation has not met its promises and commitments. The problem of intense long hours was noted by Francis Green in Chapter 4. Evidence from the psychological contract surveys supports this concern. Asked about effort, the 2000 survey shows that among those in industry:

27% said 'I am working as hard as I can and could not imagine working any harder'

37% said 'I am working very hard'

31% said 'I am working quite hard'

4% said 'I am not working particularly hard'

Higher levels of effort are consistently reported by women and effort is consistently associated with a poorer psychological contract. One reason for this is that effort is seen as externally imposed, lying largely outside the control of the worker and as such can be distinguished from the more internally driven and internally controlled concept of motivation. In other words, a further key factor for job satisfaction is the level of control over work. Those working long hours by choice are more satisfied than those who have long hours imposed on them. This sense of control over both the extent and intensity of work may not have been dealt with in the working hours legislation since it ignores the influence of organisational culture and the pressures that managers are increasingly driven to impose on their workforce (and on themselves) to compete successfully in the marketplace. Greater autonomy in work is also a means towards greater control over the pace, timing and possibly the location of work. This in turn is likely to be associated with both higher levels of job satisfaction and, equally important, higher levels of general well-being and perhaps life satisfaction.

Conclusions

It was suggested at the outset that there was limited value in asking workers what they want from work and more to be gained from assessing how they react to what they are given. Evidence of high levels of job satisfaction demonstrates that most workers have made a positive adjustment to the experience of work. Additional evidence indicates that although workers seek a balance between work and the rest of their life, a majority still view work as central to their lives. However, despite a raft of government and EU initiatives designed to improve the experience of work and despite objective indicators of improvements in the economic conditions of work, job satisfaction has tended to decline during much of the 1990s and in the past three years has at best remained stable.

One explanation for the lack of positive impact of government initiatives on worker satisfaction is that these initiatives can easily become diluted in the workplace. Yet where organisations introduce more 'high commitment' human resource practices and where workers have high levels of autonomy and involvement, levels of satisfaction and a set of other attitudinal and behavioural indicators are more positive. However, despite the rhetoric of some top managers, claiming that 'our people are our most important assets' relatively few organisations make a serious attempt to apply the practices associated with positive workers outcomes. We can speculate on the reasons for this, but evidence about the increased intensity of work suggests that they give priority to other market-driven concerns.

It is in this context that there is a role for government and for appropriate legislation. However, one of the problems appears to be that the legislation to date has had little impact on the lives of most workers. A typical example is the working hours legislation. This provides a useful lever for unions and can have an impact on the margins but it does not touch the many middle managers and professionals who work long hours; indeed, it may serve to increase the intensity of work.

In assessing what workers want from work and how they evaluate their experience of work in the years since a change of government, this chapter argued that there is value in using a concept such as the psychological contract to understand how workers appraise policies and practices against their expectations and experiences. There is clear evidence that where obligations, promises and commitments are not met, this results in a poorer psychological contract and, in turn, in lower satisfaction, commitment and motivation.

Surveys show that job satisfaction has been declining faster in the public sector and highlight particular concern in some parts of the public sector about the failure to deliver promises. There is a clear need to manage expectations, to be more realistic about what is promised and to match promises with the resources that enable them to be implemented. In the workplace, there is some evidence that good practice is more likely to be implemented where there is an established personnel function and a recognised trade union. In their rather different ways, these can both serve as necessary guardians of good practice and, in turn of workers' satisfaction and well-being.

Finally, there is some recognition that in its first term the government has placed the emphasis on improving the experience of work in the 'black holes', those small organisations with poor practices and no union presence. This is a proper priority but there are risks in ignoring the expectations and experiences of workers in those parts of the private and public sectors where evidence of declining satisfaction suggests that anticipated improvements in the experience of work are not being delivered.

References

Cully M, O'Reilly A, Woodland S and Dix G (1999) *Britain at Work as depicted by the 1998 Workplace Employee Relations Survey* London: Routledge

Blanchflower, D and Oswald, A (1999) *Well-being, Insecurity and the Decline of American Job Satisfaction* Warwick University Working Paper (www.warwick.ac.uk/fac/soc/Economics/oswald/#2000)

EPOC Research Group (1997) *New Forms of Work Organization: Can Europe Realise its Potential?* Dublin: European Foundation for Living and Working Conditions

Glynn C (2000) *Young People's Attitudes to Work, Careers and Learning* Horsham: Roffey Park.

Guest D and Conway N (1999) *Why are British Workers so Dissatisfied?* London: CIPD

Guest D and Conway N (2000) *The Psychological Contract in the Public Sector* London: CIPD

Guest D, Michie J, Sheehan M and Conway N (2000) *Employment Relations, HRM and Business Performance: An Analysis of the 1998 Workplace Employee Relations Survey* London: CIPD.

Guest D, Michie J, Sheehan M, Conway N and Metochi M (2000) *Effective People Management: Initial Findings from the Future of Work Survey* London: CIPD

Oswald A and Gardner J (2001) 'What has been happening to job satisfaction in Britain?' Paper presented to the ESRC National Conference, 28 November 2000, Updated March 2001

Rose M (2000) *How Far Can I Trust It? Job Satisfaction Data in the WERS98 Employee Survey* ESRC Future of Work Programme Working Paper 6

Wanous J, Reichers A and Hudy M (1997) 'Overall job satisfaction: How good are single item measures?' *Journal of Applied Psychology* 82,2,247-52.

7. Employee involvement and organisational performance

Mike Emmott

Involvement and participation are code words for good employment practice, but what do they actually mean? To what extent is involvement a feature of UK workplaces, and what is the evidence about its impact on business performance? In this chapter these issues are addressed against the backdrop of accumulating evidence about the economic effects of the way in which people are managed. From this analysis flows a brief discussion of the implications for public policy, and in particular how the UK should respond to proposals for an EU directive on employee information and consultation. The fundamental assumption is that public policy should be directed at supporting business performance, innovation and growth.

What are we talking about?

The language of employee involvement is notoriously treacherous. With the retreat from traditional employee relations structures and mechanisms, the terminology surrounding the relationship between employer and employee has become less familiar and more imprecise. Managers speak about fostering employee commitment; academics, (such as David Guest in the previous chapter) seek to develop alternative frameworks of analysis, based on ideas such as the 'psychological contract' between employer and employee, or 'employee voice'. These terms lack the apparent solidity of mechanisms such as collective bargaining or works councils. However they embody important insights that can contribute to improving employment practice.

Similarly 'involvement' does not refer to a specific set of practices but can be seen as embodying an aspiration or model of the employment relationship. It is used here as a portmanteau term to denote a broad range of policies or practices aimed at harnessing employees' capabilities, engaging their commitment and giving them more influence in the workplace. The intention is to avoid focusing on specific mechanisms, but to open up the broad question of what action might be taken to structure the employment relationship so as to achieve improved business performance.

The performance focus should not be seen as excluding other objectives, such as increasing employee well-being and improving the quality of working life. Most employees accept that they have a shared interest in the performance of the organisation for which they work: this is the basis for strategies based on 'partnership' between organisations and their employees. The thesis underlying 'high commitment' policies is that business performance is delivered through enlightened management practices and satisfied employees.

Consultation is defined by ACAS as 'the process by which management and employees or their representatives jointly examine and discuss issues of mutual concern. It involves seeking acceptable solutions to problems through a genuine exchange of views and information. Consultation does not remove the right of managers to manage – they must still make the final decision – but it does impose an obligation that the views of employees will be sought and considered before decisions are taken.' However, the ACAS definition blurs an important distinction between consultation directly with individual employees and indirect consultation with employees through representatives. Statutory frameworks in mainland Europe rely heavily on representative consultation, and this is reflected in the directive on European Works Councils which now applies to UK-based companies with more than a thousand employees, and at least 250 workers in two member states. Other UK legislation, particularly on health and safety, major redundancies and business transfers also requires employers to make use of representative consultation. It is, however, in the area of direct consultation – including quality initiatives, teamworking, employee attitude surveys and a range of face-to-face and other methods of communication – that most movement has taken place in UK organisations in recent years.

What is the scale of employee involvement in the UK?

For an economy-wide picture of the extent of involvement practices in the UK, we need to turn to WERS 98. Table 7.1 lists 16 frequently discussed management practices and employee involvement schemes and shows what proportion of workplaces are currently operating them. The report notes that the practices are fairly widespread, with well over half of workplaces having five or more of the 16 practices, and a fifth with 8 or more. 'Training, team-working and supervisors trained in employee relations matters and problem-solving groups are all associated with one another and might in combination be construed as a model of direct employee participation in decision-making.'(Millward *et al*, 2000)

An analysis by Millward *et al* of the WERS results from 1990 to 1998 shows in greater detail how involvement practices, and specifically consultation, have been evolving. Similar numbers of workplaces – between 80 and 90 per cent, depending on the measure used – had some form of employee voice mechanism in 1998 as in 1984, but there was a major shift from representative to direct forms of voice. Table 2 shows that the incidence of joint consultative committees at workplace level declined throughout the period. There was, however, an increase in workplaces with non-union representatives. Many workplaces continued to have arrangements combining

Table 7.1 Use of 'new' management practices and employee involvement schemes

	% of workplaces
Most employees work in formally designated teams	65
Workplace operates a system of team briefing for groups of employees	61
Most non-managerial employees have performance formally appraised	56
Staff attitude survey conducted in the last 5 years	45
Problem-solving groups (eg quality circles)	42
'Single status' between managers and non managerial employees	41
Regular meetings of entire workforce	37
Profit-sharing scheme operated for non-managerial employees	30
Workplace operates a just-in-time system of inventory control	29
Workplace level joint consultative committee	28
Most supervisors trained in employee relations skills	27
Attitudinal test used before making appointments	22
Employee share ownership scheme for non-managerial employees	15
Guaranteed job security or no compulsory redundancies policy	14
Most employees receive minimum of 5 days training per year	12
Individual performance-related pay scheme for non-managerial employees	11

Source: The 1998 WERS first findings (Table 4)

direct and representative forms of voice but the authors conclude that between 1984 and 1998 'there had been a major shift from collective, indirect and union-based voice, to direct, non-union channels'.

Table 7.2 Incidence of workplace joint consultative committees, by broad sector and union recognition, 1980 to 1998

	Cell percentages			
	1980	1984	1990	1998
Any consultative committee				
All establishments	34	34	29	29
Functioning consultative committee				
All establishments	30	31	26	23
Size of establishment				
25-49 employees	21	21	18	14
50-99	29	32	31	25
100-199	39	47	37	32
200-499	60	54	43	49
500 or more	66	70	61	58

Source: All change at work?

So WERS confirms that, although its form has changed to reflect the changing employee relations climate, employee involvement is widely practised in UK workplaces. However the report by Cully raises an issue about the depth of the involvement process. The report comments that, although two-thirds of managers said that most employees worked in formally designated teams, only 5 per cent of teams satisfied the definition of fully autonomous team-working. There was also a significant difference between the percentage of managers claiming to consult employees and the percentage of employees who believed they had been consulted. The implication is that the *quality* of involvement practices could be improved. Many managers remain sceptical about the extent to which employees feel involved in decisions affecting their jobs.

Another measure of UK practice might be how we compare with other EU countries. Because of the differences in national culture and institutions, this is not an easy assessment to make. However, an EWC Study Group supported by Fenton-O'Creevey, Wood and Callerot in 1998 found little evidence that the looser legal framework for information and consultation in the UK led overall to less activity than in member states where such practices are legally mandated. Some conclusions from a sample of large UK-owned multinationals with activities in both UK and other member states were that:

- representative committees are less important as a channel for information and consultation in the UK than in France or Germany,

- the UK has significantly higher levels of consultation on productivity and competitiveness than France and

- while UK companies showed much greater diversity in the level and mix of channels used, there were no major differences between EU countries in overall levels of employee involvement.

Given the limited number of companies in the sample (25), too much weight should not perhaps be placed on these findings but the general drift is instructive.

What are the links between direct involvement and performance?

One outstanding message to emerge from WERS 98 is the positive link between job satisfaction and the extent to which employees feel consulted about workplace changes. Nine out of ten employees reporting such consultation also said they were satisfied or very satisfied with their job: a significantly higher percentage than that produced by any other factor. If we accept that there is likely to be a strong positive link between satisfaction and performance, consultation is clearly a major contributor to business performance.

But what is the *nature* of the 'consultation' underpinning this finding? This is the key issue examined by Guest and colleagues in a subsequent analysis of the WERS data for CIPD, which concluded that 'the specific measures of negotiation and consultation do not have any consistent association with outcomes; indeed on balance they have at best a marginal impact'. On the other hand, managers in the WERS survey reported considerable growth in the importance of employee involvement and this, together with levels of informal consultation, was associated with positive employee attitudes and with some aspects of workplace performance. The authors comment that 'such findings indicate the importance of informal processes rather than the more formal and traditional industrial relations institutions for both employee and workplace outcomes'. In other words, the WERS data suggests strongly that it is *direct* rather than *indirect* forms of involvement that impact on performance.

Stark as they are, these findings should come as no surprise. They reinforce those of Gallie and others, based on the Employment in Britain survey in 1992, that in the eyes of employees:

> ...direct involvement in decisions about work organisation...is linked to higher levels of organisational effectiveness. However there is no comparable evidence for works councils, while union representation is associated with perceptions of lower effectiveness at least with respect to the planning of change.

The report by the European Works Council Study Group on employee involvement within European multinationals (referred to above) similarly found little association between formal consultation and information structures and performance. The group concluded:

> The overall story from these results seems to be that it is not predominantly the existence (or not) of formal mechanisms for informing and consulting employees that is associated with performance. Rather, it is the relationships and trust developed in these forums, and the degree to which influence over managerial decisions is ceded through them.

Does a combination of formal and informal consultation work better?

Strong support for the positive impact of direct consultation on performance comes from a major study undertaken on behalf of the European Foundation for the Improvement of Living and Working Conditions. Based on experience in 10 EU countries, the report found managers believed that all forms of direct participation had a strong impact on economic performance, and 'the more employees were informed and consulted, the greater managers thought the economic effects'. The study found a high level of employee consultation in the introduction of direct participation, though this was generally through the management chain.

While emphasising the impact of direct involvement practices, other studies have identified some reinforcing effect from combining them with indirect, representative methods. Research by Mari Sako (1997), for example, looked at a sample of UK vehicle component manufacturers and concluded that direct participation had a significant effect in reducing defects; the impact of indirect participation although visible was more modest. The most positive effects on performance were however in companies that adopted *both* forms of participation.

Millward *et al* find that employees believe managers are more responsive to employee suggestions where either non-union or direct voice mechanisms are in place, than where reliance is placed on trade union methods. However, they comment that 'the combined presence of a recognised trade union and union representation on a formal consultative committee was the only formulation to be independently associated with employees' perceptions of fair treatment by their managers'. This confirms that different forms of consultation have different effects on employee perceptions, and quite likely on performance.

Some employers clearly believe formal consultation has a beneficial impact on employee attitudes, reassuring them that their interests will not be ignored. It is reasonable to suppose that consultation on workplace change might tend to reassure employees that basic standards of 'process fairness' are being maintained (though this proposition gets little support from the Employment in Britain survey findings referred to above). The distinction here is with outcomes: it may be difficult to persuade employees that redundancy is itself fair but they can at least accept that fair principles have been applied in reaching decisions. The high levels of interest in the criteria for selecting people to be made redundant, for example, suggest that issues of process fairness play a significant part in employee attitudes to management's handling of redundancies. It remains unclear however how far consultation on redundancies has any impact on performance.

A similar story emerges from the experience of companies such as Leyland Trucks, whose participative systems are based '70 per cent on culture and 30 per cent on structure'. The company claims that organisations that fail with participation tend to stress a mechanistic approach to teamworking. Instead, Leyland periodically analyses employee attitudes and perceptions, adopts communication systems designed to ensure that each employee receives the information they need in an appropriate way, and focuses on maintaining a 'challenging but positive ethos where constructive criticism is encouraged'.

What is the impact of UK legislation requiring formal consultation?

The major source of evidence here is a study by Edwards for DTI which found that redundancy consultation tended to centre on the process of handling job losses, rather than avoiding them altogether, and did not produce perceptibly different results from management's original proposals. However, the study found that more positive outcomes occurred where management took a participatory and flexible approach. Drawing on their survey of 'partnership' companies, Guest and Peccei suggest that consultation on redundancies has less influence on management decisions than in any other area: only 1 per cent of respondents believed that consultation had 'a great deal' of influence on decisions.

Recent legislation on working time and parental leave offers employers the opportunity to adopt arrangements for workforce representation in order to vary the statutory provisions, through either recognised trade unions or elected employee representatives. However, employers have so far shown little interest in using these provisions. They offer an example of what Deakin calls 'reflexive' employment law, which combines minimum standards with discretion for local adaptation. However, Deakin himself points out that such legislation 'brings with it increased transaction costs and arguably faces severe problems of implementation in all but the smallest workplaces'. This may help to explain why employers have not shown more interest in initiating arrangements for local representation.

Where do enlightened people management practices fit in?

The broad proposition that the way in which employees are managed has a critical influence on their behaviour, and hence on workplace performance, is not now disputed. On the strength of his analysis of WERS 98, Cully for example concludes that:

> High commitment management practices are associated with better economic performance, better workplace well-being and a better climate of employment relations.

Examples of practice by individual companies strongly suggest that, although it has not been possible to show that there is a distinctive 'bundle' of practices linked to high performance, nevertheless a combination of enlightened practices is needed to deliver results. This underlines the key importance of management attitudes and workplace culture.

The research generally reports positive statistical relationships between the greater adoption of HR practices and business performance. Much evidence relates to the US but there is an increasing body of evidence (in addition to the WERS findings) relating to the UK:

- Pfeffer (1998) cites evidence that HR practices can raise shareholder value by between $20,000 and $40,000 per employee.

- A study by Huselid and Becker (1995) suggested that 'market value per employee' was strongly associated with the HR practices adopted.

- Research at Sheffield University (Patterson *et al* 1997) found that changes in profitability among a panel of over 60 small to medium sized single-site manufacturing businesses was significantly correlated with the adoption of certain HR practices.

- Thompson (1998) reported findings from an establishment-level survey of the aerospace industry that showed firms reporting higher levels of value-added per employee used HR practices for a greater proportion of their employees and were also more likely to have a board-level personnel director.

Further work in this area is currently in hand in the UK by, among others, Purcell and Guest. Although it would be wrong to suggest that any individual practice is critical, the Sheffield study by Patterson underlines the importance of (1) job design or work organisation and (2) the acquisition and deployment of skills.

What about 'partnership'?

Partnership in the UK has been enthusiastically endorsed by the TUC, as well as DTI, as a vehicle for encouraging the development of more effective employment relationships. However the study of partnership companies by Guest and Peccei found that while representative participation in *organisational policy* was associated with a range of positive outcomes for the company, representative participation in *employment decisions* was not. This reflected a 'very equivocal response to the union role, implying uncertainty on the part of both mangers and employee representatives about how unions best fit into the partnership process'. In rather similar vein, the conclusion drawn by Cully from WERS 98 is that 'it [is] not unionism per se that [is] associated with better performance, but an active union presence in tandem with high commitment management'. Although union recognition is associated with more management practices being in place, this is mostly because these practices are more widespread in large, private sector workplaces and throughout the public sector.

Using data from the British Social Attitude Survey, Bryson (1999) finds that employees see industrial relations as poor where there are recognised unions and strong on-site representation. He concludes, however, that unions have a positive influence on the industrial relations climate where

- there is a balance of power between union and management

- management is supportive of union membership, and

- employees view the union as effective.

These findings are not perhaps surprising. The historic purpose of unions has been to defend employee interests, not to support business performance as such, and the roots of much workplace machinery lie in conflict resolution. However the partnership model, supported by the new statutory union recognition provisions, leaves open the question of how union structures and behaviour can best be adapted to support a wider business agenda. The research findings can be read as suggesting both the scope for developing effective partnership arrangements, and some of the obstacles in the way of doing so.

So what is the evidence telling us?

Although the evidence is not altogether consistent, its general sense might be summarised as follows:

- although UK employers are making less use of indirect involvement practices, they are making more use of direct involvement; nevertheless take-up could be higher and more meaningful;

- there is strong evidence for the impact on business performance of a range of enlightened people management practices (referred to by Cully as 'high involvement' practices);

- there is strong evidence, based on large-scale studies and supported by managers, that direct involvement practices have a positive impact on business performance;

- there is no evidence that indirect involvement on its own has any positive impact on performance;

- the evidence suggests that a combination of direct and indirect involvement practices – voluntarily adopted by organisations – can be more powerful than either on their own;

- there is evidence for the effectiveness of 'partnership' arrangements where management seeks active trade union input, but the benefits come primarily in those (relatively few) cases where management offers a share in strategic decision-making.

What are the public policy implications of this analysis?

There is some evidence of market failure in that, despite an increased use of direct involvement methods, companies do not act in what would appear to be their own best interests by adopting *more* practices and implementing them more *whole-heartedly*. Is this a basis for Government intervention, and if so of what kind? To answer this question, we need to consider why many companies fail to gain the full benefits of good practice. No definitive answer is possible but some plausible hypotheses are:

- people management issues have not had the sustained top management interest that is applied to, for example, finance and technology;

- people management practices are difficult to apply across companies. They reflect organisational cultures, which take time to change, and require sustained management understanding and effort at all levels;

- the 'command and control' of model of management is still very influential.

Insofar as there is a public debate about involvement, it has focused on the case for legislation, and the possibility that an *EU Directive on information and consultation* will be adopted in the teeth of objections by the UK Government. The Industrial Society has recently argued that the UK should rationalise existing consultation law and oblige employers to consult employees collectively in advance about major decisions. It is suggested that we do not need to import directly the European model of consultation, but should tailor legislation (in unspecified ways) to fit UK employee relations. Sisson has also pointed out that, within the framework of the current draft directive, there is considerable scope for flexibility in both the content of the measures and how they are implemented.

However flexible an EU directive might turn out to be in practice, it is clear that it would require some means of informing and consulting employee *representatives*. This is of course the form of consultation that the evidence suggests is *least* likely to have a positive business impact. The basic problem with any form of legislation is that effective involvement must be based on trust and this can only be built on the willing efforts of both employers and employees. In the case of the draft directive, the Commission has so far made little effort to present it as a basis for improving business performance. Rather it has seen the directive as a way of resisting or delaying proposals for major restructuring involving plant closures or major redundancies, such as those involving Renault at Vilvoorde and Rover at Longbridge. A communication by Commissioner Flynn in 1995 (before either of these specific cases arose) referred to a 'strategy of prevention', which was difficult to apply when information and consultation procedures were 'isolated and limited to cases of imminent collective redundancies or business transfer'.

Against this background it will be difficult to persuade employers that there are positive business benefits to be gained from legislation. Sisson argues that effective consultation requires management to think through their decisions and get the input of employees, and that good forward planning and dialogue allow more effective management of industrial change. Similarly the interim report of a high level EU group on the economic and social implications of industrial change chaired by Pehr Gyllenhammer in 1997 said 'The challenge of industrial change will be met satisfactorily only if effective and constructive social dialogue is developed at all levels...particularly in key areas such as information and consultation of employees'. There is clearly something in these arguments but they offer little support to the Commission's specific proposals. Employers will continue to resist proposals for EU legislation that is so evidently not based on arguments about competitiveness and performance.

An incoming Labour Government will no doubt continue to endorse 'partnership', but it could recognise more clearly that this is unlikely to attract much active support from employers that do not recognise trade unions and whose employees are not interested in union membership. One method of building on and extending the partnership rhetoric could be an *ACAS Code of Practice* which could form the foundation for model procedures and practices based on the evidence of what works and showing employers how talking, listening and responding to their employees will promote business effectiveness and successful goal attainment. This would be in line with the findings of a partnership study by John Knell, which focused on 'the difficulties involved in moving an organisation from traditional command and control structures with low levels of job discretion, to one characterised by a flatter hierarchy, semi-autonomous teams, with employees being offered more meaningful control of their jobs and working time'. The contrast between such an approach, and that favoured by the European Commission, is complete.

Finally more attention could usefully be paid to *the state of the 'psychological contract'* in devising and implementing strategies to improve productivity and competitiveness. Guest has demonstrated that a positive psychological contract between employer and employee rests basically on three elements: trust, fairness and 'delivery of the deal' (the extent to which the employer's behaviour is seen to match up to the actual or implicit promises held out to the employee). There is also a strong link between the state of the psychological contract and the adoption of a range of people management practices. Monitoring the psychological contract on a national, sector or organisation basis could therefore be one practical way of monitoring progress by employers towards developing high commitment strategies and increasing levels of employee involvement, commitment and satisfaction. This is presumably one of the reasons why the DTI Company Law Review proposed last year that companies be required to include in their annual reports a new Operating and Financial Review, including an account of the company's key relationships with employees and others on which its success depends. If this proposal is to be fully effective, it will be important to make progress in devising appropriate measures.

Conclusions

The idea that there is a 'representation gap' in the UK is not one that is supported by the evidence, if the test is either business performance or employee satisfaction. Employers in the UK are interested in engaging the commitment of employees and involving them more in workplace decision-making. There is a broad consensus on what 'high involvement' practices look like, but less agreement on how extensively, and intensively, they are implemented. The wider dissemination of good practice in organisations with widely differing backgrounds and circumstances is not susceptible to 'quick fixes' or single-issue solutions. If the aim is to build workplace cultures based on trust, this requires first and foremost management buy-in, and there is little evidence that legislation can make a significant contribution here. Policies to increase competitiveness and growth should recognise the need for voluntary commitment to improving the quality of people management across the board, and give a higher priority to employee involvement and voice.

Responses to Chapter 7:
Employee and employer views

David Coats, TUC

Mike Emmott has made a heroic attempt to evaluate the evidence of the impact of employee involvement and fit this into the CIPD's view of the world – what might be described as the commonsense of the HR profession. Unfortunately, this has led to a rather partial account of the key research findings and an apparent unwillingness to accept the importance of representative participation in the policy mix that delivers high performance. Expressed most simply, the bedrock belief of the CIPD is that HR and employee involvement make a difference and trade unions or works councils do not. A good employer can achieve more through the application of progressive HR than through a high trust relationship with a trade union. This explains the view often expressed by CIPD officials that if an employer does not recognise a union today there is no reason why they should do so in the future – and why the Director-General of the CIPD was so vociferous in opposing the procedure for statutory trade union recognition.

Is there a representation gap?

A casual reader of this chapter might also assume that widespread consultation and effective employee involvement can be found in the majority of British workplaces. Extensive reference is made to the WERS findings which, on closer reading, reveal that in most workplaces employees have little or no scope to influence management decisions affecting the future of the organisation. For example, fewer than a fifth of employees reported frequent consultation about workplace change. Seventeen per cent said that they were asked their views on changes to future work practices and fourteen per cent on plans for the workplace. The lowest levels of participation related to issues like redundancy (eight per cent) and pay (five per cent). WERS makes clear that there is a representation gap in the majority of British workplaces and confirms the finding from the 1990 survey that:

> Britain is approaching the position where few employees have any mechanisms through which they can contribute to the operation of their workplace in a broader context than that of their own job. There is no sign that the shrinkage of trade union representation is being offset by a growth in other methods of representing non-managerial employees' interests and views. (Millward, 1994: 133)

Direct and indirect participation

Emmott's argument is rooted in the notion that institutions do not make a difference and he adduces evidence from the EPOC survey and the EWC Study Group report to support his case that statutory obligations on information and consultation cannot legislate high trust relationships into existence. This latter point could be seen as a statement of the obvious – just as the benign intervention of a Family Division judge cannot save a marriage that is heading for divorce – but it ignores the role of the law in establishing basic norms that all employers must comply with. Similarly it fails to understand that the law is intended to change employer behaviour and act as a spur to increased employee involvement.

Contrary to Emmott's assessment both the EPOC and EWC studies are clear that institutions do matter and that trade unions or works councils cannot be ignored in developing public policy. The key finding from the EPOC survey is that:

> Far from being barriers to progress, it seems, employee representatives are the agents of change. The greater their involvement in both form and extent (and this applies to negotiation and joint decision making) the more the indicators of the effects were positive. (EPOC, 1997)

Summarising the findings of their EWC study in People Management, Wood and Fenton-O'Creevy (1999) draw attention to two conclusions: first, those organisations that relied only on direct involvement involved their employees less than those using other systems; second, although unions tended to be used as a channel for a limited number of issues, the level of involvement was higher on average in unionised operations. Their most significant general finding is that:

> [E]xclusive reliance on direct involvement is likely to lead to lower levels of overall employee involvement and lower productivity (Wood and Fenton O'Creavy, 1999, p45)

The results published in the 1999 OECD Employment Outlook confirm that unions or works councils generate pressure for greater management innovation through the introduction of flatter management hierarchies, team working, job rotation and broad employee involvement strategies (OECD, 1999).

In sum then, the evidence points to high performance resulting from a complex of practices involving representative participation (through trade unions or a works council) and a high level of individual employee involvement.

Public policy implications

It is difficult to understand how a full appreciation of these studies can be used to rebut the argument for statutory works councils in the UK. Indeed, adherence to the principle of evidence based policy making would lead the UK government towards enthusiastic support for the proposed EU directive instead of the current outright opposition. The WERS findings drive any neutral reader to the conclusion that exhortation has not worked and, in the absence of statutory obligations, most employers will continue with minimal and rather ineffective consultation on a narrow range of issues.

A law establishing UK works councils could be supplemented by precisely the kind of good practice guide that Emmott recommends and an enhanced DTI Partnership Fund focused on promoting workplace innovation. In the absence of this more sophisticated approach a good practice guide, however excellent, will simply gather dust on the bookshelves of HR managers.

Don't forget that workers are citizens too

The argument for consultation advanced so far has been instrumental – consult and you will get good performance – but a much stronger case can be made for information, consultation and participation on ethical grounds. How people are treated in the workplace tells us something about the kind of society we live in, about the relationships we have with each other and the extent to which citizens are treated as autonomous individuals whether at work or at leisure. The argument has been well expressed by Joseph Stiglitz, former chief economist at the World Bank:

> We care about the kind of society we live in. We believe in democracy. Democratic processes must entail open dialogue and broadly active civic engagement, and require that individuals have a voice in the decisions that affect them, including economic decisions...Economic democracy is an essential part of a democratic society. (Stiglitz, 2000)

Dominic Johnson, CBI

The CBI strongly supports employee involvement as a matter of voluntary good practice. As Chapter 7 shows, direct employee involvement – especially when reinforced by indirect – is beneficial for both business and employees. It can improve staff satisfaction, buy-in to decisions and even the bottom line. Trade unions and the European Commission have called for new law in this area, based on the four arguments discussed below. But the proponents of statutory intervention have misunderstood the nature of employee involvement. Situations of collective redundancy and business transfer aside, employee consultation is a matter for business, not government. Government's role, if there is one at all, is straightforward: simply to support the development and dissemination of the business case for effective employee involvement.

The usual supporting arguments

Proponents of new law have tended to argue that:

- Emotive and high profile cases of industrial restructuring like the Vilvoorde closure have shown that – due to a *lack of law* – employers can ride rough-shod over employees' sensibilities when making redundancies.

- Employee involvement delivers *business benefits* and, ultimately, long-term competitive advantage. Employers need to be forced to do this by law because they haven't done it for themselves.

- Businesses that avoid effectively involving their employees have an unfair advantage over those that take a good practice approach. There needs to be a *level playing field*.

- Just as citizens have rights to a voice in decisions affecting them in a democracy, so *employees have rights to a say in decisions affecting them in the workplace*.

But these views are not well founded.

- For a start, there is already robust consultation law. The high profile cases of large-scale redundancies that underpin calls for new law have all been governed by the Collective Redundancies Directive. New law would go no further on job losses than its already strict provisions. Where more than 20 redundancies are taking place consultation has to begin 'in good time' and with 'a view to reaching agreement' on proposals. And this cannot be lip service to a *fait accompli*. Proposals must be tabled while they are still at a 'formative stage', including an examination of whether redundancies are necessary. Clearly, in some cases these obligations have not been well observed. But this makes the case for better guidance and enforcement of the existing law. There's no case for introducing new law that duplicates measures already in place.

- A strong business case is an argument against the need for new law. If consultation helps deliver long-term competitive advantage, as Emmott suggests and proponents of new law emphasise, then there is no need to legislate – because the market will take care of it. Those firms that have good people management practices (including effective consultation) will perform better than those that don't, and consultation will spread by the 'Invisible Hand' of its own success.

But what if the market hasn't worked yet? Shouldn't companies be forced to 'take the medicine' of consultation? The idea of using legislation to make companies do the things that may be good for them is wrong-headed. Whether companies manage well or not is a matter of competitive advantage: it separates successful companies from the unsuccessful. By the logic of the proponents of new law, we should legislate in every area – from people management to capital investment – where companies don't do things that might make them more successful. But the law is too crude an instrument for making companies manage well. Such law creates a compliance approach, as we have seen in some cases with the European Works Councils Directive: you can lead a horse to water but can't make it drink. A much better approach is to promote the business case and guidance to persuade companies to consult and involve employees as a matter of enlightened self-interest.

- The level playing field argument is contradictory. Logically, proponents of new law cannot simultaneously argue that employee involvement delivers business benefits and that businesses that don't consult are likely to undercut those that do. Either, consultation gives an advantage to businesses, in which case there is no issue of firms stealing a march on each other and therefore no need to introduce minimum standards law. Or employee involvement is a net cost on businesses, but something that they ought to do because society attaches a value to it, in much the same way as governments regulate, for instance, maternity law. Which takes us to the core argument underpinning calls for new law on employee involvement – employee rights.

- The belief that democratic rights to a voice in decision-making extend to the workplace is superficially attractive. Its rhetorical force comes from the anger people understandably feel when collective redundancies are mishandled. But the unpalatable truth is that a company is not a democracy. The assets of a company are owned by its shareholders, who employ management and workers to deliver returns on their behalf. Clearly employees have an interest in how their company is run, and any sensible management ought to respect and value their views. But this is a matter internal to the company. Where employees do have a right to a voice in decisions that affect them – currently, in the case of business transfers, large scale redundancies and transnational issues – the law is premised on the existence of economic externalities in which government and society has an interest, for instance the effect of job losses on a regional economy. Such externalities are not obvious in relation to ongoing employee involvement in normal business operating conditions.

References

ACAS (1997) *Employee Communications and Consultation*

Barnard C and Deakin S (2000) 'In search of coherence: social policy, the single market and fundamental rights' *Industrial Relations Journal*

Bryson A (1999) 'Are unions good for industrial relations?' in *British Social Attitudes: the 16th report* National Centre for Social Research

Burns P (2000) *The Silent Stakeholders* Industrial Society

Cully M, Woodland S, O'Reilly A and Dix G (1999) *Britain at Work: as depicted by the 1998 Workplace Employee Relations Survey* Routledge

EPOC Research Group (1997) *New Forms of Work Organisation: Can Europe realise its potential?* European Foundation for the Improvement of Living and Working Conditions

Fenton-O'Creevey M, Wood S and Callerot E (1998) *Employee Involvement within European Multinationals* EWC Study Group,

Gallie D, White M, Cheng Y and Tomlinson M (1998) *Restructuring the Employment Relationship* Clarendon Press

Guest D and Peccei R (1998) *The Partnership Company: Benchmarks for the Future* Involvement and Participation Association

Guest D, Michie J and Sheehan M (2000) *Employment Relations, HRM and Business Performance: An analysis of the 1998 WERS* CIPD

OECD (1999) 'New Employment Work Practices and Their Labour Market Implications' *Employment Outlook*

Oliver J (2000) 'Participation and Culture at Leyland' *IPA Bulletin* December

Knell J (1999) *Partnership at Work* DTI Employment Relations Research Series 7, Department of Trade and Industry.

Millward N (1994) *The New Industrial Relations?* London: Policy Studies Institute

Millward N, Bryson A and Forth J (2000) *All change at work? British employment relations 1980 -1998, as portrayed by the Workplace Industrial Relations Survey series* Routledge.

Richardson R and Thompson M (1999) *The Impact of People Management Practices on Business Performance: A literature review* IPD

Sisson K (2000) 'Why UK Ministers should support an EU consultation directive' *EWC Bulletin*

Stiglitz J (2000) *Democratic Development as the Fruits of Labour* address to the US Industrial relations Research Association, Boston, January 2000

Wood S and Fenton-O'Creevy M (1999) 'Channel Hopping' in *People Management* November

8. Work-life policies: where should the government go next?

Lisa Harker and Suzan Lewis

Work-life issues are not new. Generations have striven to reconcile the demands of employment and family life. What is new is the prominence of work-life issues in public discourse and the extent to which these are being addressed in public policy-making. The management of paid work and family life has long been considered a problem for individual women, or at best, families, to resolve. Increasingly it is recognised that workplaces have to change to reflect employees' work-life needs, and that both the state and employers are stakeholders in this process.

To date most employer initiatives to address these issues have taken the form of so called 'family friendly' policies that are seen to be marginal to strategic business issues. While new policies and practices have enabled some individuals (mostly mothers) to combine employment and caring, fundamental culture change in the workplace has not occurred.

A lack of clarity about responsibilities acts as a barrier to cultural change. Where do employers' responsibilities for the balance of individual's lives begin and end and what should the state be responsible for ensuring happens? For government a number of overlapping (and potentially competing) rationales for what has been termed work-life balance policies have emerged and in order to determine the priorities for the future direction of government policy in this area a clearer framework is required.

Government action on work-life balance must also be informed by what is effective in bringing about change. To date, the Government has regarded its role to be supporting and reinforcing a family friendly culture in business, with voluntary measures needing to be underpinned by a statutory framework. But this approach is based on a number of assumptions. It assumes that there is a relationship between government actions (including both statutory rights and stimulation measures) and employer actions. It rests on the belief that it is possible to identify and promote good practice in relation to work-life balance and that the promotion of the business case for change is the best way of persuading employers to implement the necessary changes. These assumptions are rarely tested.

Rationales for government action on 'work-life balance'

Governments have long been involved in work-life balance issues. The principle motivations for government involvement have been improving business performance, safeguarding the welfare of mothers and children and encouraging equality of opportunity.

New Labour has promoted work-life balance policies in relation to each of these rationales, but the most dominant rationale has been improving business performance. In the 1998 Fairness at Work White Paper (DTI, 1998), work-life balance policies were put forward as being important for competitiveness because they ensured that companies had the biggest pool of potential employees from which to draw.

The government's approach has been to attempt to win the hearts and minds of business, to 'support and reinforce' a family-friendly culture (DTI, 1998), to encourage employers to go further than the new statutory minimum framework of work-life balance rights, by convincing companies of the 'business case' for introducing work-life balance practices.

The business case rests on the argument that enabling individuals to combine their caring and employment responsibilities has performance benefits, because it allows companies to attract a wider range of skilled employees, enables skilled employees to remain in work (and to work more effectively) and brings additional corporate benefits, such as good publicity.

While the government's approach is clear, questions still remain as to the appropriate scope of the minimum statutory rights introduced by government, such as which groups of employees should be covered by the statutory minimum rights and where the line should be drawn between statutory minimum rights and good practice. The concern among businesses that an ever-expanding statutory framework may emerge is fuelled by lack of clarity about the likely scope of statutory minimum rights.

This also raises the question about whether the other rationales for introducing work-life balance policies should be given more weight in the development of future policy. For example: should government policy be seeking explicitly to reduce gender inequalities in the balance of home and work life, prioritise statutory rights for those with dependants or improve the quality of life of all employees?

In establishing a framework for work-life balance policies which is likely to bring about the kind of cultural change needed, the government needs to balance each of these priorities.

Welfare of dependants

So far little public policy attention has been paid to the impact of a carer being in work on the welfare of the dependant (with the exception of maternity benefits policy), although the research evidence is mixed and controversial.[1] But work-life balance policy could be more orientated towards ensuring that the best interests of a dependant (the child or disabled or elderly person) are met. Key issues might be the importance of both mothers' and fathers' involvement during the first twelve months of a child's development (Kendall, 2001), the importance of male and female role models for children, or the impact of changing caring patterns on children or adult dependants, including the elderly or those with disabilities.

To-date work-life policies have paid comparatively little attention to the needs of those caring for an adult dependant. Carers of both types of dependants share the similar work-life balance needs: flexibility in order to combine paid work and caring and support in terms of the additional service and cost requirements of looking after a dependant.

In addition, policy debates have tended to overlook the fact that individuals may move in, out and within different caring roles over the life course: any one person faces the likelihood of having both childcare and adult dependant responsibilities during their working life. If, instead, we consider how best to support individuals of working age as they move in and out of their caring roles over the life course, the distinctions between carer and non-carer, childcare and adult carer become blurred. This is important both in terms of gaining broad support for policy change and signalling the relevance of carer-friendly policies to men as well as women. As much as half the working-age population has some caring responsibilities: there are approximately 13 million parents with responsibility for at least one child under the age of 18 and some 4 million adults with responsibility for an adult dependant in the working-age population.[2]

There are, however, differences in the extent of dependency of children and adults and arguably a stronger rationale (that is one which rests on safeguarding the future of society) for the state to intervene in relation to the former. The state needs to signal where it stands on this matter, but if work-life balance policies were driven by an objective to safeguard the welfare of dependants they would:

- ensure that the minimum right to leave from work or flexible working patterns to care for a dependant was informed by the needs of dependants

- prioritise help with work-life balance for those who have responsibility for looking after an adult or child dependent.

Equal opportunities

Despite the fact that around 45 per cent of the workforce is made up of women, there is a considerable gender divide in relation to work-life balance. Fathers' employment rates exceed mothers' by around 10 per cent. Mothers spend three times as much time caring for children or elderly dependants as fathers.[3] Household chores are shared equally in only 35 per cent of dual-earning couples, with women undertaking the bulk of chores in the vast majority of households (Ferri and Smith, 1996).

Women are most likely to have child caring responsibilities. Their working patterns continue to be affected by these responsibilities, whilst those of men are largely unaffected. By contrast, the gender differences are less marked in relation to caring for an adult dependant.[4]

If a primary objective of work-life arrangements is gender equity, this requires that pluralistic ways of working are valued equally with traditional work patterns so that employees who pursue flexible careers have equal access to advancement (Raabe, 1996). A gender equity approach also implies the need for fairness and equity in the distributions of rewards and constraints in both work and family domains (Fletcher and Rappoport, 1996). There is a need to challenge ways of working which fail to recognise the interdependence of paid work and family for men and women. As gender equity in the workplace cannot be separated from gender equity in the family, organisations may also need to confront gendered processes beyond the workplace, for example, encouraging men to take their share of family leave for sick children.

A number of commentators have noted that in focussing on the work-life balance needs of women at the expense of men, policies could entrench gender inequalities (Brannen, 2000; Moss, 2000; Reeves, 2000). Improving maternity leave in the absence of paternity leave, for example, merely reinforces gender differences. Employers frequently target policy (explicitly or implicitly) on women rather than men (Forth et al, 1997). Even the introduction of parental leave – open to mothers and fathers – is unlikely to reduce gender inequalities unless it is paid sufficiently high to encourage men to take it (Demos, 1997).

Research suggests that employees are reluctant to demand work-life balance policies (Lewis, 1997; Burkitt and Edwards, 2001). The existence of work-life balance policies does not, in itself, led to their take-up. However the demand for, and take-up of work-life balance policies is particularly low among men, despite the fact that many report that they would like to be able to spend more time with their children.[5]

A cultural change is needed in order for men and women to feel entitled to ask for, and take-up, work-life balance policies. Government is right to say that it has no role in telling people how they ought to live their lives[6] but in order to ensure that men and women have a genuine choice as to how they want to share caring and domestic responsibilities, they must face a level playing field at work. Culture change will not come about by statutory legislation alone – but establishing rights for men as well as women sends a powerful message.

If work-life policies were driven by an objective of addressing gender inequalities they would:

● place greater emphasis on establishing minimum rights for fathers to take time off work to look after children (through paid parental leave and the introduction of paternity leave[7])

- discourage employers targeting work-life policies on women (and encourage them to extend provision to men) – In this context, it might be possible to strengthen anti-discrimination law.

- seek to generate public debate about the value of more equal sharing of caring responsibilities

Quality of life

Ultimately the work-life balance agenda will be undermined by one thing: the unwillingness of society to change. In the context of long working hours, dominated (in culture if not in practice) by a full-time model of employment, those who seek to work reduced working hours will always be more likely to face discrimination in terms of prospects and pay.

The work-life balance debate has sought to embrace the idea that such policies are needed for all those in society not just parents (or, more specifically, mothers). Yet the vast majority of government action in this area is focused on support for parents. Is this justified?

Employment has an impact on the lives of individuals, particularly in the face of limited resources or long working hours. A legitimate goal for public policy would be to try to ensure that work does not undermine a person's quality of life: including avoiding being detrimental to family relationships or an individual's mental health.

Although the impact of work on quality of life is far from straightforward, and one person's quality of life can be different from another's, there are issues of concern. There is accumulating evidence that long hours of working are linked with stress related symptoms (Sparks *et al*, 1997) which not only affect people at work but also spillover to affect home life and family members (Westman and Etzion, 1995). Stress accounts for 14 per cent of sickness leave and the annual cost of stress to the UK is estimated to be as much as £5.3 billion (ILO, 2000).

The work-life balance agenda needs to embrace the bigger challenges of improving quality of life. Clearly, though, these are changes which governments alone can not bring about. In the short term the government needs to articulate a vision for work-life balance which is both ambitious in seeking to improve quality of life for all, but also clear about the immediate priorities for state support.

Making the business case – does it work?

Despite clear evidence that some employers have benefited from introducing a work-life strategy and some evidence of a link between job satisfaction, good HR practices and company productivity (West and Patterson, 1999), the business case does have limitations.

Firstly, the evidence base remains weak: most studies of the business case are based on a small sample of case studies of mostly – although not entirely[8] – of large companies. For example, Shirley Dex and Fiona Scheibl found 'evidence of productivity increases from family-friendly policies in at least eleven organisations and a further six organisations reported morale and motivation improvements'. (Dex and Scheibl, 1999) – typical sample sizes in this area of research. Since the business case will be different in each organisation, case studies are perhaps the best form of evidence. However, there is still a need for more extensive evidence across different sectors. It is not yet possible to prove that the business case holds across all industries. One would expect the business case to be weaker, for example, in sectors with low margins, or where there is a surplus supply of labour.

Secondly, the business case is not overwhelming even in examples where work-life balance policies have been adopted. For example, Forth *et al* found that only half of providers of family-friendly policies reported improved morale/staff relations and only one-quarter reported easier retention of staff, enhanced loyalty or improved performance/motivation (Forth *et al*, 1997). Similarly Cully *et al* found that only 50 per cent of companies they researched reported happier staff, 36 per cent reported an increase in retention of employees and 24 per cent a reduction in absence levels (Cully *et al*, 1999). It can be difficult for employers to identify a clear relationship between the introduction of work-life balance practices and improved company performance (or an avoidance of a decline in performance), particularly in the short term.

If work-life practices are developed to address the specific needs of organisations (the nub of the business case argument), rather than as a response to social expectations about basic rights and facilities, it follows that provisions will be diverse and may not reflect the needs of all employees. There is much discussion of win-win solutions, which benefit organisations and employees, but the business case implies that it is the needs of the business, which take priority. In practice, however, employers do not take the business case to extremes. Some employers do introduce work-life policies that benefit employees (and their families) and are *not detrimental* to their business, as well as those that *benefit* their business.

Overall the business case for introducing work-life balance policies has not been so compelling as to convince the majority of employers to make substantial changes to working practices. While there may be gains to be had from articulating the business case more effectively to companies, experience in other countries suggests that the business case will not be sufficient to ensure that all workers benefit from work-life balance policies. The reality is that some businesses, particularly small firms, far from embracing the business case argument, fear the impact of such policies on business performance and use this reason for not doing so.

If the welfare of children and others needing care is of genuine concern, and in the absence of strong regulation, the business case needs to be tempered by a corporate social responsibility argument. A corporate social responsibility approach would shift the perspective from a short-term business case to a longer term one. For example, rather than focusing on a decline in sickness absenteeism, a longer-term business case would be to focus on improvements in the wellbeing of employees- high morale, absence of unnecessary stress, commitment to the company. The criteria for successful corporate social responsibility would include societal as well as individual and business outcomes, ie win-win-win solutions.

Who suffers from the limitations of the business case?

Although it is not possible to be precise, the current failure of the business case could affect a significant proportion of employees. Two-fifths of managers interviewed in the 1998 Employee Relations Survey reported that flexible working arrangements were not available to non-managerial employees. Only one in five mothers returning to work are entitled to a wide range of voluntary benefits from their employees, two-fifths are entitled to a medium range of benefits, a quarter to a narrow range of benefits and an eighth to no benefits. One in five (21 per cent) of fathers have no entitlement to any kind of benefit (Forth et al, 1997). Employees most likely to lose out are those in small, private sector companies with no union representation (Harker, 1998).

Convincing more companies of the business case will reduce the number of employees losing out but there are clear signs of an emerging inequality which the government needs to address. At the onset of parenthood, a clear polarisation emerges between highly educated, high wage mothers who are likely to remain in work and lower educated, low wage mothers who are more likely to leave the labour market. Only one in three women with net household incomes of less than £500 a month return to work compared with nearly nine in ten women with monthly incomes of more than £2,500 (Callender et al, 1997). Similar patterns of inequality have emerged in other countries (Lewis, 2000).

There could be a number of reasons for this inequality but the absence of work-life balance policies is likely to be one. Most women who do not return to work after childbirth say this is because they wish to look after their child themselves (Callender et al, 1997). Other reasons frequently given are the lack of affordable childcare and unsuitable working hours. Aside from low labour market orientation, the difficulty of managing work and family time may not be compensated sufficiently by an adequate income. Those earning lower incomes may well be working in companies which are least convinced by the business case.

There are other groups whose chances of being in employment are comparatively low, for whom lack of work-life policies might be a disincentive to work. Employment rates for lone mothers lag significantly behind employment rates for other parents; around half of lone parents with dependant children are in work. The risk of worklessness among carers of adults is also high; 49 per cent of adult dependant carers give up work due to their caring responsibilities.[9] Problems reconciling work-life demands may also impact on other groups. Only 46 per cent of the disabled are in work, compared to 80.3 per cent of the rest of the working age population and one in three of the 50-60 (or 65) population are not in work (see Chapter 2).

Government action: what works?

Legislation, regulation and public provision

There has been much debate about whether government action through the establishment of rights and public provision encourage firms to implement voluntary policies and practices by communicating the message that families are valued, or simply absolve employers from having to address further work-life issues. One way to inform this debate is to compare the prevalence of work-life policies in different national policy contexts.

In the United States, where state supports are minimal and work-life is regarded as primarily a corporate issue (Gonyea and Googins, 1996), work-life policies and practices are often highly developed in leading-edge companies. The same is true of Australia and Japan where there is also a limited infrastructure to support work-life balance. However provisions are patchy in these countries.

Public sector organisations and large private sector corporations in specific sectors are most likely to provide such arrangements. In addition, highly skilled workers are more likely than other employees to be offered such arrangements, although they are also the workers most likely to be subject to the expectations of the long hours culture (Evans 2000).

Thus, while some employers may offer a wide range of work-life arrangements there are many employees who have access to little or no support for managing employment and other responsibilities. Furthermore, in the US, Australia and Japan, as in Britain, there is a long hours work culture, which undermines any provisions available.

Access to work-life support appears to be more evenly spread when it is based on statutory rights. Although organisational size and sector influence the provision of voluntary employer work-life policies across EU states, as elsewhere, there are also national differences, which suggest that policy context does make a difference, albeit not always in the expected direction.

Studies suggest that voluntary provisions by companies are highest in countries with a medium level of statutory provisions (such as Austria and Germany) and least likely in those countries with the lowest levels of statutory provisions (such as UK or Ireland) or in those with the highest levels of support (for example, the Nordic countries) (Evans 2000).

It is possible that national legislation tends to encourage private provision up to a point, after which it tends to replace it, although it must be recognised that both public policy and the behaviour of firm's behaviour are conditioned by cultural attitudes toward the family (Evans 2000).

Evidence of higher levels of statutory provision associated with lower employer provision may partly be an artefact of survey data collection. National surveys of employer policies tend to focus on childcare support, and family leave beyond the statutory minimum, rather than flexible forms of work, and policies which are less relevant in the Nordic countries where public provision of childcare is high and statutory leave rights are generous. The need for employers in countries with a higher level of statutory provision to accommodate statutory family leave arrangements may actually oblige employers to develop flexibility in working patterns (Kivimaki, 1998).

There is therefore some support for the view that the establishment of rights and provision by national government can encourage the development of voluntary initiatives in organisations up to a point, and that without such action many employees, including those who are most in need, are likely to be excluded from work-life provisions. Although the extent to which more extensive government action encourages or discourages employer responses remains unclear, it does seem that a higher level of entitlements for working families than currently available in Britain may encourage greater employer provision.

Promoting good practice

It is important to be clear about what constitutes good practice. DfEE guidance (DfEE, 2000) defines good practice as 'adjusting work patterns so that everyone, regardless of age, race or gender, can find a rhythm that enables them more easily to combine work with their other responsibilities and aspirations'. Importantly, this focuses on diverse needs, not just those of women with young children, and refers to the adjustment of work patterns for all rather than family friendly policies.

Most of the examples of good practice offered by government demonstrate win-win solutions for employees and business. In the short term it may be important to define good practice in terms of mutually beneficial solutions, in order to gain the support of business. But ultimately other objectives need to incorporated into our definition of good practice – relating to gender equality, the welfare of dependants, and quality of life.

The Government's approach is to provide employees with a floor of entitlements while also encouraging employers to implement voluntary additional entitlements and develop good practice. Examples of encouragement and stimulation measures include: DfEE information highlighting the business case for organisational change; efforts to model good practice as an employer, and the Challenge Fund to support work-life consultants in selected organisations. What evidence is there that such measures can influence employers?

There is almost no research on this topic and we can only seek to draw lessons from existing practice. Cross-national comparative studies do suggest that stimulation measures by governments can influence both the prevalence and focus of employer work-life arrangements when promotion of good practice is accompanied by incentives. A study of work-family arrangements among large service sector organisations in the Netherlands and Britain found that Dutch employers were far more actively involved in the field of childcare than British employers. Seventy per cent of employers surveyed reported having adopted some form of childcare support compared with 27 per cent of British employers surveyed (Den Dulk and Lewis, 1999). This was thought to be the result of an initiative introduced by the Dutch government in 1990, which included the provision of subsidies and tax breaks and created an organisational structure characterised by public-private partnerships.

If the goal of work-life policy making is to encourage genuine choice for more people and to see fundamental change in workplaces, then sense of entitlement and actual take-up will be a more important indicators of the success of government strategies than just workplace policy implementation.

Implications for government policy

The limitations of the business case have both short-term and long-term implications. In the short term the government needs to take action to ensure that those who lose out because of the limitations of the business case are still able to effectively balance their home and work commitments. In the long term there needs to be a more fundamental change in corporate culture so that businesses support all employees with their work-life commitments for reasons not limited to the business case.

There are two different (and not entirely mutually exclusive) routes for government in the short term. Either it could seek to establish a statutory minimum rights framework which is sufficiently comprehensive to ensure that all employees (whether working in a 'family-friendly' company or not) are able to effectively combine work and family life. Or it could seek to target support at those individuals who are currently most likely to lose out because of the limitations of the business case.

Whether by introducing a more comprehensive minimum standard, or by targeting eligibility for support, government policy needs to ensure that the following particularly 'at risk' groups do not lose out:

- employees in small companies

- employees on lower incomes

- the most 'at risk' social groups: lone parents, carers, those over the age of 50 and those with disabilities

Establishing a comprehensive statutory minimum rights framework akin to that implemented in the Nordic countries raises the question of whether or not this would stifle or encourage employer action (and therefore long-term corporate cultural change). We do not yet have the full answer to this question, but given the UK's starting point it would appear that further statutory provision is unlikely to stifle employer action. There is nevertheless considerable distance between the current UK statutory work-life framework and that in Nordic countries.

A targeted approach, which would seek to prioritise statutory support for certain groups, is not without difficulties, however. Such an approach might backfire, by creating a disincentive for employers to take on certain 'at risk' employees if the work-life balance costs attached are not sufficiently compensated. There is already momentum building around the notion of a backlash against those who have entitlement to work-life provision.[10]

What is certain is that, in the short term at least, failure to address the limitations of the business case will result in greater inequality, which is, in itself, ultimately a threat to productivity. In the short term, the government might need to consider a combination of a medium-level statutory minimum rights framework, with targeted support for employers and employees to address the business case limitations. This might consist of:

- a framework which establishes minimum rights relating to each of the key challenges associated with establishing work-life balance: temporary absence from work, the need for flexibility in working patterns and the support to help meet the costs associated with caring responsibilities. Such a framework might include paid leave arrangements (including parental and paternity leave), flexible working rights (including a right to work reduced hours) and support with the costs of caring (eldercare as well as childcare tax credits?).

  plus

- targeted support for those groups currently not benefiting from the business case. This might include, for example, a grants programme specifically aimed at encouraging small businesses to adopt work-life balance policies and additional financial support via the benefit/tax credit system for those in the most marginalised groups seeking to work part-time (for example, lone parents, carers, those over the age of 50 and those with disabilities).

Conclusion: the future direction of policy

The work-life balance agenda has been dominated by promoting the business case and while this has been important in promoting employers' good practice, it has underplayed its limitation and failed to address the particular problems of those who do not benefit from it. In addition the case for introducing work-life balance policies which respond to the needs of dependants, encourage greater equality between men and women and, ultimately, seek to improve quality of life for all, has been overlooked.

Three key lessons emerge from the existing evidence:

● Government encouragement or stimulation of employer work-life arrangements can be effective, particularly if this involves some financial incentives, but it is necessary to be clear about what constitutes good practice.

● The business case alone is unlikely to bring about the levels of change needed for long term social and economic benefits. Corporate social responsibility should be encouraged alongside the business case.

● If there is genuine concern for the welfare of families, it may be appropriate for Government to extend financial incentives to those firms who might incur some costs in implementing work-life arrangements.

A more robust framework for work-life policies and practices is needed which has at its core a set of statutory minimum rights which address all aspects of the difficulties which individuals face balancing work and other life commitments. This core also needs to reflect the needs of dependants and the need for men as well as women to benefit from work-life balance support.

Such a framework might include:

● paid parental and paternity leave (as announced in Budget 2001)

● a right to work reduced hours

● leave policies which are informed by the needs of dependants

● statutory work-life measures which are open to men and women equally

In addition there is the need to articulate the case for targeting support on those who are least likely to currently benefit from employers' good practice. This might include particular measures to support small businesses or those particular groups who are least likely to benefit from the business case. However this has to be done in the context of setting out a longer-term goal for achieving better quality of life for all. Cultural change should be promoted by government through, for example, seeking to generate public debate about the value of more equal sharing of caring responsibilities and of the unacceptability of gender bias in employers' work-life provision. The success of the work-life balance agenda will ultimately be judged in terms of the quality of life of citizens rather than the number of state or employer work-life policies that have been introduced.

Ultimately the business case will retain some importance, particularly if employers take a long-term view. However, employers also need to develop a sense of social responsibility if cultural change is to occur. A major question for the future is how we can best encourage, whether by regulation or by voluntary agreement, a broader view that basic standards of good employment should include the right to reconcile work and family life.

Endnotes

1   For a review see Dex S (ed) (1999) *Families and the Labour Market: trends, pressures and policies* Joseph Rowntree Foundation/Family Policy Studies Centre.

2   The 1995 General Household Survey found that 6 per cent of 16-29 year olds, 10 per cent of 30-44 year olds and 20per cent of 45-65 were looking after a sick, handicapped or elderly person. On current population figures this suggests 4.2 million adults care for an adult dependant. Of these, 60 per cent care for someone with a physical disability, 7 per cent with a mental disability and 15 per cent with both a physical and mental disability. Most care for an elderly person: 71 per cent of those cared for are aged 65 or over.

3   About 1.2 million women work as well as looking after an elderly relative. Women spend an average of 1.56 hours a day caring for children and adults; men spend an average of 0.54 hours a day (*Social Focus on Families* ONS, 1997).

4   The differences in caring roles for men and women are less striking in relation to adult dependants: 14 per cent of women care for an adult dependant compared to 11 per cent of men (1995 General Household Survey).

5   A MORI poll found that 66 per cent of men say they would be likely to take paternity leave (May 2000); see also Burghes L, Clarke L and Cronin N (1997) *Fathers and Fatherhood in Britain* Family Policies Study Centre.

6   Speech made by Stephen Byers at 'New Ways to Work' conference, May 2000

7   The 2001 Budget announced the introduction of two weeks' Paternity Leave in 2003, paid at the same flat rate as Statutory Maternity Pay.

8   *Family Friendly Employment: The Business Case Report* DfEE

9   *Caring Costs: the time costs of caring* Carers National Association, July 1996

10   Elinor Burkett, who has written extensively upon the situation of contemporary women within the US, has recently published *The Baby Boon: How Family Friendly America Cheats the Childless* (March 2000).

References

Brannen J (April 2000) *The societal consequences of changing gender roles: employment, care and citizenship* unpublished paper

Burkitt N and Edwards L (2001) *Wanting more from work? Aspirations and expectations of people in low and middle paid jobs* DfEE Research Brief RBX 6-01

Callender C, Millward N, Lissenburgh S and Forth J (1997) *Maternity rights and benefits in Britain 1996* DSS Research Series 76

Cully M, Woodland S, O'Reilly A and Dix G (1999) *Britain at Work: as depicted by the 1998 Workplace Employee Relations Survey* Routledge

Den Dulk L and Lewis S (1999) *Factors influencing work-family arrangements in the UK and the Netherlands* Ninth European Congress on Work and Organisational Psychology: Symposium on Community, Work and Family, Helsinki

Dex S and Scheibl F (1999) 'Business performance and family-friendly policies' in *Journal of General Management* 24.4

DTI (1998) *Fairness at Work*

DfEE (2000) *Creating a Work-Life balance: A Good Practice Guide for Employers*

Evans J (2000) 'Firms contributions to the reconciliation between work and family life', Paper presented at the Conference on Families, Labour Markets and the Well Being of Children, University of British Columbia, Vancouver

Ferri and Smith (1996) quoted in Dex S (1999) *Families and the labour market: trends, pressures and policies* Joseph Rowntree Foundation/Family Policy Studies Centre

Fletcher J and Rappoport R (1996). 'Work-family issues as a catalyst for organizational change' in Lewis S and Lewis J (eds) *The Work-Family Challenge: Rethinking Employment* Sage Publications, London

Forth J, Lissenburgh S, Callender C and Millward N (1997) *Family-friendly working arrangements in Britain 1996* DfEE research report, RR16

Gonyea J and Googins B (1996) 'The Restructuring of Work and Family in the United States: A New Challenge for American Corporations' in Lewis S and Lewis J (eds) *The Work-Family Challenge: Rethinking Employment* Sage Publications, London.

International Labour Organisation (2000) *Report on stress and mental illness in the UK, the United States, Germany, Finland and Poland*

Kagan C, Lewis S and Heaton P (1998) *Caring to Work: Accounts of Parents Combining Employment with Care of Disabled Children* Family Policy Studies Centre

Kendall L (2001) 'Pregnant mums should get child benefit' *New Statesman* 12 February

Kivimaki R (1998) *How work is structured by the family? The impacts of parenthood on the work community* Paper presented at the Gender, Work and Organisation Conference, Manchester

Lewis S (1997) 'Family Friendly Policies: Organisational Culture Change Or Playing Around At The Margins' *Gender, Work And Organisation* 4 13-23

Lewis S (2000) *Changing Workplaces* Paper for IPPR seminar November 2000

Lewis S and Lewis J (1997) 'Work family conflict. Can the law help?' *Legal and Criminological Psychology* 2 155-167

Moss P (2000) 'Modest hopes or Great Expectations?' in Wilkinson, H (ed) *Family Business* Demos

Raabe P (1996) 'Constucting Pluralistic Work and Career Arrangements' in Lewis S and Lewis J (eds) *The Work-Family Challenge: Rethinking Employment* Sage Publications, London

Reeves R (2000) *Mothers versus Men: why women lose at work* The Industrial Society.

Sparks K, Cooper C L, Fried Y and Shirom A (1997) 'The effects of hours of work on health: a meta-analytic review' *Journal of Occupational and Organisational Psychology* 70 4 391-408

West M and Patterson M (1999) 'The workforce and productivity: people management is the key to closing the productivity gap' *New Economy*

Westman M and Etzion D (1995) 'Crossover of stress, strain and resources from one spouse to another' *Journal of Organizational Behaviour* 16 169-181

Wilkinson H, Radley S, Christie I, Lawson G and Sainsbury J (1997) *Time out: the costs and benefits of paid parental leave* Demos

9. Training in work – the evidence

Francis Green

In the closing stages of the last Conservative administration, Britain's training system was described by a Labour spokesman (soon to be a government minister) as a 'disgrace'. The sentiment was widely shared and searching for improvements to Britain's skill formation system has been a major focus of the government since 1997. It is also one of the key priorities of the union movement. This chapter briefly summarises the key evidence on the amount and distribution of training that takes, as a background to Mark Corney's discussion of policy options in the following chapter.

Training in work is everyone's idea of a 'good thing.' It is subject to market failures but it is possible that these can be resolved better elsewhere. Policy solutions must depend on a clear understanding of the training system and what the problems are. This chapter argues that:

- Britain's chief problem lies in its relatively lowly qualified labour force compared to similar industrial nations, especially at the intermediate level.

- It is not just a supply shortage issue: employers are not requiring large sections of the workforce to have qualifications, especially at the intermediate level.

- Britain's initial education and training system still lags behind other countries: flows of well qualified young people into the labour market remain relatively poor.

- But, with regard to continuing training, on average Britain has performed well: adult employees in Britain are as likely to receive training as those in comparable countries and although there is unequal access to training, Britain is not alone in having this problem.

Initial and continuing training

In assessing Britain's skill formation system we need to distinguish the system of continuing vocational training (CVT) – or more broadly, work-related life-long learning – from the system of initial skill formation through education and quasi-apprenticeship training. In terms of sheer volume, Britain does *not* have a problem with its continuing training system. There is as much, and often more, work-related training taking pace amongst adults in Britain as in most other industrialised countries (Figure 9.1). There is also evidence of a good deal of work-based skill acquisition that is not derived from training as such.

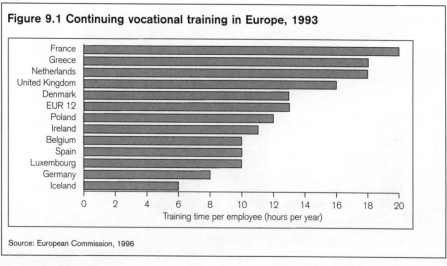

Figure 9.1 Continuing vocational training in Europe, 1993

Training time per employee (hours per year)

Source: European Commission, 1996

Rather the problem lies with its initial skill formation. The British labour force is relatively lowly qualified compared to similar industrial countries such as France and Germany, especially at the intermediate level (Table 9.1). This lead the National Skills Taskforce to recommend, as one of its key targets, increasing the proportion of 25 year olds with a level 3 qualification from 41 per cent to 70 per cent by 2010.

Table 9.1 The supply of intermediate qualifications: international comparisons

	Level 2+			Level 3+		
	UK	France	Germany	UK	France	Germany
25-28 year olds	66	83	85	41	54	78
Total workforce	55	73	83	37	36	74

Level 2 refers to five or more higher graded O-Level/GCSE passes or the vocational equivalent; Level 3 refers to two or more A-level passes or the vocational equivalent.

Source: National Skills Task Force (2000).

However, this is not simply a problem of the workforce failing to meet employers demands. Employers are not requiring large sections of the workforce to have qualifications. This is especially true at the intermediate level; nearly half of the workforce hold an intermediate qualification, but just over a third of current jobs require workers to have them (Figure 9.2). At the bottom end of the labour market, there are many more jobs that do not require qualifications than there are workers without them. In other words many people have qualifications which are not used or required in their job.

Britain's initial education and training system still lags behind others. Participation in post-compulsory education is significantly lower in the UK than in many other

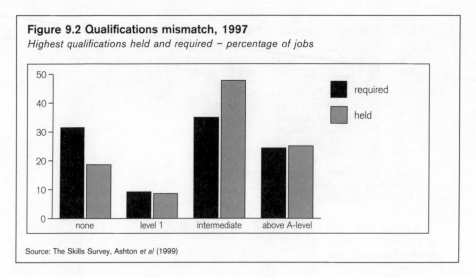

Figure 9.2 Qualifications mismatch, 1997
Highest qualifications held and required – percentage of jobs

Source: The Skills Survey, Ashton *et al* (1999)

European countries, with a comparable proportion of 17 year olds staying in education, but far fewer 18 and 19 year olds. Despite improvements since the 1980s Britain's gains are slowing down and there is no evidence that its stock of skills is approaching that of other economies. Arguably, the initial skills gap is widening.

Outcomes from training

Britain's CVT system appears to perform quite well in terms of quality. Although it is hard or impossible to benchmark training quality against other economies, there is evidence that training does help to significantly raise people's skills, to give them further qualifications and to lift their wages. Training is also instrumental in raising levels of employee commitment to organisations. In short, work-related training in Britain does contribute significantly to the quality of working life, at least for those who have good access to it.

There is robust statistical and qualitative evidence that training raises skills (Felstead *et al*, 1997): 9 out of 10 employees are positive about their in-work training experiences, reporting that in their view their skills had increased as a result. Those skills are also for the most part transferable: Of those whose skills were raised, 9 out of ten report that the new skills they acquired would be transferable to another employer. Around 43 per cent of work-based training episodes are part of a process of studying for a qualification of some sort. The importance of certification has slightly increased since the 1980s, when the equivalent figure was around 39 per cent (Green, 1999).

Estimates of the gross return to employer-based training are generally positive. In Britain they range from 5 to 15 per cent, implying that wages are higher by these amounts compared with those who have and those who have not had training (Blundell *et al*, 1996). However, these figures do not measure the return to investment in training since they do not take costs into account. The majority of the costs of training (including direct payment of costs and provision of time) are borne by employers. Only about 10 per cent of training is purely sponsored by employees. The rest is down to employers only (63 per cent) or some mixture of employer, government and employee.

There is some limited formal statistical evidence and abundant informal evidence that training raises employees' commitment to the organisations they work for. To take one example, roughly 35 per cent of large firms report that the training they provide for their sales staff has the effect of increasing enthusiasm for their corporate objectives (Felstead *et al*, 1997). In this sense, training can be seen as part of the range of 'high commitment' management practices described in Chapters 6 and 7. On average, training has little impact on job mobility, despite employer fear about trained staff being poached by rivals and so losing their investment.

Access to training

Nevertheless, there is a big problem with the continuing training system in terms of its failure to address the comparative exclusion of already disadvantaged groups from further skill acquisition. Although the training system cannot itself be blamed for economic and social exclusion, it does little to minimise it and in some respects aggravates the problem. The key factors that determine whether a worker is likely to be trained or not are first and foremost prior education and occupation and secondly firm size, age, job tenure, and the presence of a trade union in their workplace.

Employees who already have qualifications are far more likely to receive training at work than those without. There is also a clear gradient, with participation in training rising with the level of qualifications held. Using evidence from the British Household Panel Survey, 70 per cent of those with no formal qualifications had no training at all over a five year period, compared to 40 per cent of those with O-levels, and less than a quarter of graduates (Figure 9.3). A similar pattern is shown for occupational class. Seventy per cent of those in unskilled jobs had no training over a five year period, compared to just over a quarter of managers and a fifth of professionals (Figure 9.4).

Critically, those employees most vulnerable to potential unemployment receive very little training. Figure 9.5 shows that people in unskilled and partly skilled jobs are not only less likely to receive any training than professionals, managers or non-manual workers, they are less likely to have received training that would be of use for a future job. These are the same people who have the highest likelihood of becoming unemployed. So the system of training in work is hardly in a position to assist in raising the employability of employees where it is most needed.

Finally, although it is clear that there is a major problem of inequality in access to training in work, it is worth asking whether Britain has a particular problem in this area. The tendency for employers to invest in the training of more highly skilled and

Figure 9.3 Exclusion from training over 5 years by qualifications (%)

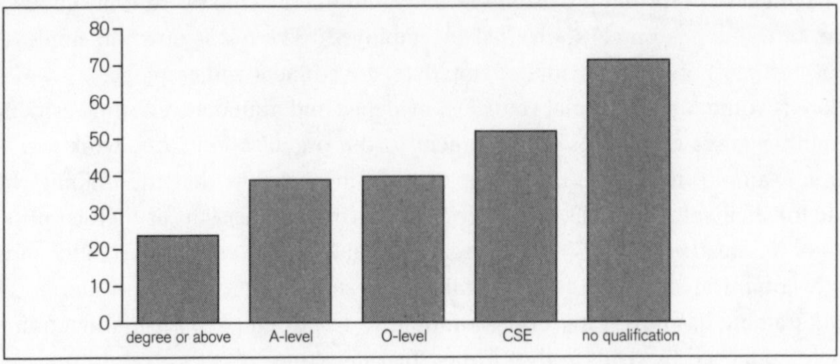

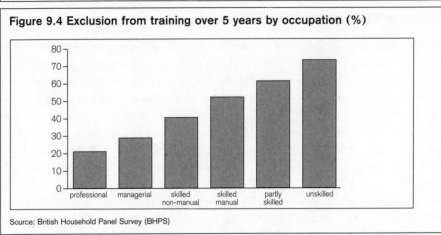

Source: British Household Panel Survey (BHPS)

Figure 9.4 Exclusion from training over 5 years by occupation (%)

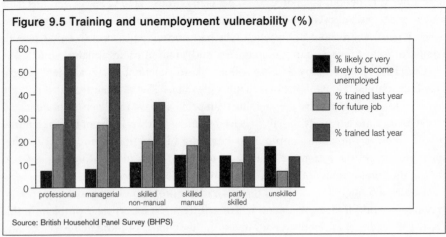

Source: British Household Panel Survey (BHPS)

Figure 9.5 Training and unemployment vulnerability (%)

Source: British Household Panel Survey (BHPS)

qualified staff – because the returns are higher- is likely to be universal. On the evidence that is available, it does not seem to be the case that access to training in Britain is especially unequal. Data from the International Adult Literacy Survey show the differential between training participation by the highest and lowest educated groups in a number of countries. On this measure, Britain is a middling performer. It has a greater gap than Sweden, where the lowest educated workers have a participation rate which is 75 per cent of that of the highest educated, but a smaller gap than the US, where the proportion is closer to a half (Figure 9.6).

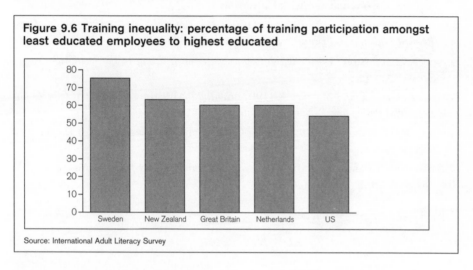

Figure 9.6 Training inequality: percentage of training participation amongst least educated employees to highest educated

Source: International Adult Literacy Survey

Summary and policy implications

To sum up, Britain's training problem is worst at the initial level; there is not enough skill acquisition in the immediate post-school period taking place. Employers are not carrying out less continuing training than comparable countries, but exclusion from education and training in this crucial early period is not being corrected in adult life.

It is unlikely that the volume of continuing training in the UK is going to rise greatly, and unrealistic to expect CVT to resolve the economic problems associated with Britain's low skill base. The main push has to come through initial skill formation, by further expanding participation in post-compulsory education and training. Doing the latter might also help, over time, to broaden access to employer-provided CVT. In the meantime, it is unlikely that training access will become less unequal. Currently, many employers do not find it profitable to provide continuing training for most of their lower-skilled workers. Although trade unions have, in the past, been a significant force for raising and broadening training, in the absence of a major renaissance for unions, wider access to training will continue to rely on individual initiatives backed where appropriate by the state (public and personal initiatives). In Chapter 10, Mark Corney looks in detail at various policy options open to the government.

References

Ashton D, Davies B, Felstead A and Green F (1999) *Work Skills In Britain* Oxford, SKOPE, Oxford and Warwick Universities

Blundell R, Dearden L and Meghir C (1996) *The Determinants And Effects Of Work Related Training In Britain* Institute For Fiscal Studies

European Commission (1996) *Key data on vocational training in the European Union* Brussels

Felstead A, Green F and Mayhew K (1997) *Getting the Measure of Training Centres for Industrial Policy and Performance* University of Leeds

Green F (1999) 'Training the workers' in Gregg P and Wadsworth J (eds) *The State of Working Britain* Manchester University Press

National Skills Taskforce (2000) *Skills for all: Research Report from the National Skills Taskforce* DfEE

10. Employer-based training – the policy options
Mark Corney

Francis Green's discussion of Britain's training effort in the previous chapter suggests that we do not have a particular deficit compared to other countries in the amount of work-related training. The problem is a lack of initial skills among people entering the world of work, and inequalities in access to training for people in work. However, the extent to which there is a 'training gap', is open to question, and the relative priority that should be given to different social and economic goals is a political choice. The important thing for policy makers is that they are clear about the overall policy objectives. Any major new interventions or legislation must be based on agreement about what the problem is that we are trying to solve.

What are the objectives?

We need to distinguish between the goals of widening participation in education and training, increasing employability (for unemployed people or those already in jobs), and increasing financial and time investment in training. There are choices to be made about the relative contribution of the State, individual and employer to each of these objectives, and how much we want each to increase its investment in education and training. There is also a strong case for differentiating between particular types or sizes of employer.

Supply and demand side

Another key distinction to be made is between supply side measures and demand side. Training policy specialists too often concentrate on employer-facilitated training in isolation from wider people management and business strategies. Policies are generally designed – wittingly or unwittingly – to increase the supply of skilled workers or workplace learning opportunities. Equally important, however, is the role of product, innovation and employment strategies in driving-up employers' skill demand. These in turn can be influenced by business support and policies, especially for small and medium-sized enterprises. At the same time, existing opportunities for training and development offered by employers or government are not always taken up. This raises the question of whether this is due to barriers such as lack of time or resources, or whether more attention should be paid to individuals' demand for them.

Employer training in context

This chapter sets out some of the options for post-16 education and training policy, to provide an overall framework to analyse future policy approaches and specific interventions. It begins with a series of ways of strengthening the current voluntary approach, and then outlines possible statutory frameworks. Finally, it puts these options into the context of wider welfare reform and employment relations policies.

The voluntary approach

There are a number of reasons why policy makers might want to retain a voluntary approach and increase efforts to strengthen it. They could:

- believe that it delivers the best policy outcome;

- believe that it delivers the second best outcome but retain it because they cannot devise an statutory approach which works; or

- they might be able to devise a statutory approach that works but still retain the voluntary one because it would cut across current and future policies with a higher political priority.

Why individually-driven strategies?

Within the voluntary approach, there are decisions to be made about the balance between policies focusing on individuals and on employers. It is worth setting out some of the reasons why policy makers might plump for individual focused strategies compared to employer focused strategies.

On a practical level it is difficult to contact, and then penetrate, three million employers, most of which are Small and Medium Enterprises (SMEs). The stock of SMEs is also not static, and their interest in training is often linked to whether they are growing and have strong innovation and product development strategies. In a flexible labour market, there is a case for individuals to take greater responsibility for investment in transferable skills and qualifications to maintain their employability.

Specific strategies targeted on individuals might include increasing awareness of state support for learning, increasing individual purchasing power, and increasing individual financial investment through loans and savings vehicles. Irrespective of the overall policy balance, the publicly funded post-16 education and training system is a crucial policy lever at the disposal of decision makers within a voluntary framework. Changes could be made to funding mechanisms and the system of maintenance allowances, as well as refocusing current spending on tuition funding.

Employer-based strategies

If employer-based strategies are to be used, policy makers must decide what mix of academic and vocational education they are seeking to create. Do they want a system where almost all young people enter full-time academic and vocational education, with employers and individuals funding adult training including adult apprenticeship, master and graduate level training? It could be that instead they want a minority – say 20 per cent – to enter youth apprenticeships, or even 50 per cent, as under the German system.

Employer-based strategies also need a clear definition of 'workforce development' and an exposition of the role that employers should play in it. Unfortunately, the term is so nebulous that the number of definitions in use is as long as a piece of string. Typically, the narrow definition of it (in England) refers to employer funding of training (£15bn-£20bn per annum) plus public funding of training, especially Foundation and Advanced Modern Apprenticeships (£0.9bn per annum), NVQs and Investors in People. Wider definitions add the post-19 adult learning budget of the Learning and Skills Council (£2bn). This chapter is based on a definition which encompasses publicly funded post-16 education and training; employer funded training outside the publicly funded system, and also welfare-to-work policies designed to engage the future workforce including the unemployed and non-employed.

Defining employer involvement in workforce development

Employers' involvement in workforce development can include a number of different practices, coming from different motivations. Clearly they will only invest resources (including management time) if they expect a return to the business, but this benefit does not have to be immediate or clearly identifiable. The expected gains can include general improvements in employee satisfaction, which can translate into better organisational performance in the longer term. Three key distinct elements are:

- *workplace learning* – where an employer decides to allow employees and their families to use company facilities such as IT equipment and training rooms to participate in learning;

- *employer funded training and learning* – where employers fund on-the-job and/or off-the-job provision, which might include voluntary time-off for study, because they believe there will be a direct benefit – in full or in part – to their organisation, and

- *employee development opportunities* – which are either integrated within, or external to, existing personnel and training practices, and provided by employers themselves or jointly with other employers because they believe that such opportunities can creates a more flexible, adaptable and committed workforce.

The focus here is on the role of employers in meeting their own workforce development needs. Key policy levers and options to strengthen employer driven strategies include:

- the use of publicly funded post-16 further education and training, and higher education to influence and meet the employer skill needs;

- the use of indicative planning to influence funding allocations over and above individual learning choices;

- extending access to public subsidies to increase company training planning including the achievement of Investors in People;

- placing training on the bargaining agenda, and

- strengthening business support and competitiveness strategies to drive-up skill demand.

A fuller set of possible options is set out in Figure 10.1, p157-158.

The statutory approach

Despite the extensive list of potential policy levers and policy options targeted on employers, policy makers should not underestimate the difficulty in strengthening voluntarism. Furthermore, they should not underestimate the task of devising a more robust voluntary system of employer investment in training and employee development. Figure 10.2, p159-160, provides a list of the main options for statutory measures focused on employers.

The National Skills Task Force (NSTF), which reviewed post-16 further education and training policy and reported in July 2000, agreed on a set of 24 recommendations, but was split on the case for a stronger statutory framework. Some of the Task Force members of the Task Force argued that the present voluntary system, strengthened by the recommendations, would not create the necessary skilled workforce to match those of our competitors. In the words of the *Final Report*:

> …it is essential that a statutory framework is created that, through a system
> of tax incentives and, where necessary, tax penalties, ensures that the
> training issue is placed on every company's agenda. The facility should exist

for such a framework to be established on a general or sector basis, so that sectors where there is consistently ineffective training performance could be targeted. (NSTF, 2000: Para 4.56).

The final response to the Task Force from the Secretary of State for Education and Employment was published in February 2001. He explicitly ruled out statutory measures to force employers to train their staff.

> I do not propose, and the Taskforce did not recommend, the introduction of a stronger statutory obligation on employers to train. I believe that in a modern economy, we must look at a more imaginative set of levers that help ensure employers make the right decisions about the importance of skills and developing people to their business.

> As part of this I am ready to use existing powers...to provide statutory backing for proposals in any sector for collective skills investment, provided the social partners agree there is clear evidence of a skills deficit and that this is the bets way forward. This already happens, for example, in the construction and engineering industries, where employers support the raising of collective funds to support the sector's training needs through Industry Training Boards (ITBs) It is why we will continue to provide backing to underpin their work.(DfEE, 2001, Para 48-49)

The response also ruled out the Task Force's recommendation that the Investors in People (IiP) standard should be supported by offering tax relief to firms that achieve it. However, the White Paper on Enterprise, Skills and Innovation, produced by the DfEE and DTI and launched at the same time, proposed to consult on 'how to give statutory backing to the network of Union Learning Representatives' (DTI/ DfEE, 2001, Para 2.42) who act as workplace experts to promote access to training and education courses. As part of the goal of 'extending opportunity for all in work, particularly to obtain a qualification up to level 2' (5 GCSEs at grade A-C), the 2001 Budget also stated that the Government was 'willing to consider' a new tax credit for training, possibly based on the model of payable Research and Development tax credits (HM Treasury, 2001).

Given this position on training levies and on learning representatives, it is worth examining other ways government could strengthen employer training provision. It could looking more carefully at flexible training levies; possible ways of introducing them are set out below. On the other hand, if it believes that even flexible options are undesirable, and that what is needed is empowerment for individuals, it could look at rights to time off to study for employees. This might help rebalance the distribution of training at work in Britain. This approach could be backed up by the Union Learning Fund, which could have more resources allocated to it.

Options for flexible training levies

In any strategic discussion of training levies, consideration must be given to the following general design features:

- the extent to which medium, small and micro businesses are covered by levy arrangements;

- the type of levy arrangements and the choice between levy-grant and remissible levy systems;

- the rate of the levy and the choice between a common rate or a differential rate between size of employer.

Figure 10.3 (p160) sets out the options for flexible training levies. Given the emphasis on policy flexibility, this chapter assumes that levy options which allow greater choice over these general design features will be viewed more favourably than levy options where these arrangements are predetermined.

Options 1-3 would fall under the category ruled out by Secretary of State for Education and Employment in 2000. Against the benchmark of developing options for flexible sector training levies, Option 4A falls well short. Such an approach would certainly be flexible in terms of covering identified rather than all sectors, but the Secretary of State would be imposing a levy without empowering the sector to have a say in the general design features set out above. By contrast, 4B at least seeks to trade-off the imposition principle – there will be a levy in identified sectors – against the empowerment principle – giving identified sectors an opportunity to design the levy arrangements.

The underlying principle of Options 5A-C is, to varying degrees, is obligatory consultation. Option 5A represents the hard version of the obligatory principle to the extent that every sector would be obliged to conduct a statutory and regular ballot to introduce or not a levy. Option 5B represents a slightly softer version in the sense that every sector would be required to conduct a one-off rather than a regular ballot. On the other hand, Option 5C is based on the Secretary of State imposing a one-off or regular ballot on identified under performing sectors.

The advantage of Options 5A-C is that they combine obligatory consultation of varying degrees with the empowerment principle of giving sectors an opportunity to design the levy arrangements. A key issue, however, is the make-up of the constituency which will be able to vote on the question of flexible levies, and whether in particular the constituency should be solely employers, and employer members of national training organisations or trade associations. It could be argued that one of the by-products of obligatory consultation via ballot arrangements with members of national training organisations or trade associations could boost their membership.

The underlying principle of Options 6A-B is voluntary agreement. Option 6A calls for a pro-active approach by the Government to encourage sectors to introduce voluntary agreements for training levies. Option 6B is a slightly stronger version of the voluntary agreement principle in that a sector wishing to introduce a training levy could request a statutory underpinning by the Government.

Options 6A and 6B combine the voluntary agreement principle and the empowerment principle. Clearly, such approaches must be based on each sector deciding upon the type of levy based suited to them. That said, these approaches are unlikely to encourage a rush of sectors to introduce a training levy. Sectors can introduce a voluntary levy at present and could ask the Secretary of State to use powers under the 1982 Training Act to establish a statutory training levy.

Options for statutory paid study leave

Current arrangements

In September 1999, 16-17 year olds in employment received a new Right to Time Off for Study or Training.[1] This could be extended to other age groups or different levels of qualification. The existing legislation covers people who are not receiving full-time education or training, and are without an initial Level 2 qualification (academic, general vocational or work-based). It covers all employers who have employees aged 16-18 and there is no qualifying period of employment. It entitles 16-17 year olds to:

- time off with pay, to study any type of qualification – academic, general vocational or work-based – within the national qualifications framework;

- free tuition with learning courses funded by the State and not employers;

- reasonable time-off which although not defined in detail: a) takes into account the requirement of the course in question and the effect of the employee's time off on the running of that business, and b) is equivalent to up to a day per week which could be spread throughout the working week, on a part-time basis or on a block release basis, to avoid busy times of the year;

- entitles 16-17 year olds to appeal to employment tribunals.

The right covers 16-17 year olds but also 18 year olds if the entitlement has already been exercised and more time is needed to complete a course, and allows study at the workplace, elsewhere on site, with a training provider, another employer, at a college or a combination of these

At the end of 1997, there were an estimated 110,000 16 and 17 year olds in England in employment and not qualified to Level 2 and not working towards a Level 2 qualification. Most were employed in small firms (fewer than 25 employees) in key sectors such as manufacturing; retail and motor trades; hospitality and other service sectors.

Government policy at the time noted the connection between right to study and the National Minimum Wage. Certainly, the same employees in the same small firms in the same sectors would have been doubly affected if the NMW had applied to 16-17 year olds. In the event, the Government decided to exempt 16-17 year olds from the NMW.

A preliminary evaluation of the right (DfEE, 2000) identified a number of barriers to take-up. It found that for young people the main barriers appeared to be: lack of awareness of the right; apprehensiveness of approaching the employer; a lack of self-confidence amongst low GSCE achievers, and the fact that some were undecided about their future career and relevant learning or training. Barriers for employers appeared also to include lack of awareness of the right to study, as well as a tendency not to see the need for training beyond induction level, opposition to the notion of non-job related study or training, and misconceptions about the right. For the careers service/TECs, take up appeared to be limited by the fact that converting employers to training through face-to-face contact is resource intensive, as well as the right to study not being seen as a high priority. There were also some misconceptions of right to study as a programme rather than a right. Other barriers identified were the age limit on eligibility inflexibility of training provision.

The preliminary study concluded that

> Although take up of financial assistance available in respect of right to study has been low it is believed that the introduction of the legislation has had a significant impact on take-up of Foundation and Advanced Modern Apprenticeships and furthermore there are signs that the direct impact may be growing...Although it may take time to effect the cultural change, which the legislation promotes, it is possible that more significant direct outcomes might be achieved in the near future. In particular, and having been able to promote right to study to Year 11 students throughout the whole of the 1999/2000 academic year, some careers services/TECs expect to see more interest from young people when college courses start in September.

Extending the right to paid study leave

If the right to study were to be extended beyond 16-17 year olds, there are a large number of variables that could be altered. These include the age range, qualifications level, type of learning (just vocational or any kind), amount of time off and learning providers covered. The split of the costs of learning between state, individual and employer is crucial, as is the remuneration during time off- whether it is paid, at what rate and by whom. The current policy includes state funding of full tuition for an initial Level 2 qualification, employer funding of full wages, and involves employers dealing with loss of an employee and production.

In order to make the analysis easy to manage, here it is assumed that all employers will be covered by any future extension of right to paid study arrangements. It also assumes that the key variables to mix and match are the age of employee, and qualifications between basic skills and an initial Level 3. Some of the more interesting potential extensions from the position at the end of the 1997-2001 Parliament are set out below:

- 16-17 year olds achieving an initial Level 2 plus all remaining employees achieving basic skills;

- 16-17 year olds achieving a Level 2 and/or all remaining employees achieving a Level 2

- 16-19 year olds achieving a Level 3 and all remaining employees achieving basic skills

- 16-19 year olds achieving a Level 3 and all remaining employees achieving a Level 2

Essentially, Option 1 combines the current arrangements for 16-17 year olds with the suggestion of Sir Claus Moser to extend the right to paid study to those without basic skills. Option 3 represents a double extension of the current arrangements, and would ensure that the right to paid study leave would underpin the statutory tuition entitlement for 16-19 year olds as set out by the Learning and Skills Act, combined with the Moser proposals for adults without basic skills. Option 4 would ensure that the right to paid study leave would underpin the statutory tuition entitlement for 16-19 year olds as set out by the Learning and Skills Act, combined with a publicly funded tuition entitlement for adults to achieve an initial Level 2 qualification, as proposed by the National Skills Task Force.

On balance, Option 3 and 4 are, perhaps, worth considering in further detail. Clearly, both would increase the proportion of employees covered by right to paid study leave, and as a consequence, increase the cost of compliance to employers, especially to small businesses. With respect to generalised models of right to paid study leave, it is important that policy makers seek to address the problem of cost of compliance to employers. This might be addressed by measures such as retaining the condition that the State pays the full cost of tuition and linking right to the achievement of vocational qualifications or vocational qualifications linked to the business or sector within which the employer operates. Wage costs to employers could be reduced by requiring the State to cover the cost of wages during study leave in full; creating a system of shared costs between employers and the State, or linking employer wage costs to the development rate of the National Minimum Wage. A framework for the various statutory options is set out in Figure 10.2.

However the key issue for employers, especially small businesses, is the loss of workers time and the sheer inability to recruit staff cover. Time not wage costs is the most critical problem with generalised right to study models.

Given this analysis, a generalised entitlement to paid study leave could only be considered under conditions where a significant proportion of the wage costs are met by the State or regulated downwards. An innovative recruitment service would be needed to assist small firms to obtain staff cover. It would also depend on there being no policies elsewhere which could increase significantly the labour costs of small businesses or increase time off by their employees.

Political priorities and policy options

The options for flexible training levies and paid study leave described above might have an impact on training and learning outcomes but have manageable consequences for the business community. However, policy makers need to judge the options for flexible training levies and statutory paid study leave against existing and future employment relations policies. Outside the field of collective rights, since May 1997 the Government has implemented:

- the Working Time Directive – October 1998;

- the National Minimum Wage – April 1999;

- the Parental Leave Directive – December 1999, and

- the Part-Time Working Directive – April 2000.

The room for manoeuvre in the area of training will be affected by moves to extend or introduce maternity, paternity and parental leave over the coming years, as well as by the extent of the impact on small businesses of rises in the National Minimum Wage.

Taking the right to paid study leave, increases in the NMW and parental leave policies together, it is clear that there are implications for regulatory costs to employers in terms of the administration of rights. The NMW increased wage payment costs to some employers, and study, parental and Paternity leave involve potential loss of staff. These costs all have impacts on small businesses. It is worth noting though, that if maternity leave payments are to be increased, and allow women to take longer breaks from work for childbirth, the costs to businesses are not necessarily greater. Arranging cover for a staff member can be easier for a year than a few months, and the marginal cost of cover can fall after the initial recruitment and training. However, finding replacement staff may prove difficult in a very tight labour market, which the UK has and would hope to have in the future. The creation of a new public/ private partnership between the Employment Service and private sector recruitment agencies will be critical in this respect, as the DTI Green Paper on Parents and Work (DTI 2000) makes clear.

Opportunities for statutory training policies in the wider context

One of the key issues to bear in mind is the extent of overlap between state paid parental or paternity leave and any extension of the right to study. The objective would be to minimise the overlap to avoid a position where a large number of employees are taking paid parental leave combined with a large number of other employees taking paid study leave. This leads to the conclusion that, assuming family leave entitlements are increased, the least degree of overlap would be young people because they are least likely to have young children.

The right to paid parental leave might be compatible with the right to paid study leave for 16-19 year olds to achieve an initial Level 3 qualification (discussed above as Options 3 and 4). However careful consideration would have to be given to a system based on the right to paid parental leave and the right to paid study leave for adult employees without basic skills, and/or employees without an initial Level 2 qualifications.

There are a few policy options that might help reconcile the rights. Government could consider the extent to which a formal learning entitlement might be incorporated within the paid parental leave entitlement. This might require a change in the wording and meaning of the parental leave regulations. Another option would be to consider the extent to which parents could be sign-posted to family learning opportunities such as family learning centres, and to personal lifelong learning opportunities such as access to Learn Direct and Individual Learning Accounts. The Campaign for Learning has explored the links between paid parental leave and family learning (CfL, 2000).

The tentative conclusion from this analysis is that in the context of expansion of family leave, the right to paid study could be extended to 16-19 year olds but not extended to adults. In this area, the best approach would be to sign-post adults with rights to paid parental leave to family and personal learning opportunities offered by the DfEE, Learning and Skills Council and University for Industry.

Finally, there is the issue of where options for flexible training levies might fit in with this framework. On balance, it could also be argued that the options for flexible sector levies, especially 5A-6B (see above), could be accommodated within an uprating of the NMW, the greater leave entitlements for parents and extended paid study leave to 16-19 year olds.

Conclusion

There are a wide variety of options open to the government in the field of training, both in terms of strengthening the existing voluntary system, and by adding to it with new statutory measures like flexible training levies or rights to study leave. However, it is vital that policy makers are clear about what they are trying to achieve, and what the problem is in the first place.

The various interventions described here could be used to increase the supply of skills to the economy, to help workers retrain, or to increase individuals' employability. The desire to tackle inequity in access to training and development opportunities will not always pull in the same direction as the desire to tackle the economy's skill shortages, or the needs of businesses. If the 'business case' for intervention is to be reconciled with the social justice case for greater access training for working people, training has to be promoted as a part of employers overall strategies, not as an add-on.

Endnote

1   This was implementing Part III of the Teaching and Higher Education Act 1998 in England and Wales

Table 10.1 Policy levers and options for employer-driven strategies

Developing a more relevant qualifications system	developing a qualifications system which allows for progression and transfer between and across the academic, vocational education and work-based routes from Level 1 to Level 5
	incorporating basic skills and key skills within work-based qualifications
	developing full-time part-time Foundation Degrees underpinned by existing tuition and maintenance arrangements
Increasing demand for publicly funded work-based training	ensuring teachers and careers advisers explain the benefits of the work-based route to pupils aged 11, 14 and 16
	encouraging small and medium-sized employers to participate in Foundation and Advanced Apprenticeships
	encouraging local LSCs to target tuition subsidies to SMEs rather than large companies
	reducing wage costs of trainees by the use of voluntary sector-based wage agreements
Strengthening the training infrastructure	encouraging colleges and universities to specialize in vocational areas
	reviewing the NTO network and providing adequate public funding to them to conduct permanent and long-term skills foresight programmes
	creating a standard and capital fund for non-college providers perhaps on a loan basis rather than a grant basis
Targeting public funding on skill needs	allowing the LSC network to allocate 16-19 funding to meet long-term skill needs, thereby reducing the budget for 6th form schools and colleges if necessary and increasing funding to the work-based route
	targeting an increasing share of additional funding to higher education to vocational sub-degrees
	directing a significant proportion of the LSC adult learning budget to employer skill needs
	providing regional development agencies will direct funding to shape the allocation of 16-19 and post-19 provision
Increasing awareness of the benefits of organisational training outside of publicly-funded training	developing a marketing campaign to demonstrate the benefits of organisational training to employers
Improving company training planning	offering tax credits to SMEs going for Investors in People
	the extent to which the Ufl learning content can assist SMEs to introduce basic training plans

Increasing the pay back to employers of investment in training	encouraging employers to use the Development Rate of the National Minimum Wage to reduce wage costs during the initial training period
	issuing employers with best practice and legal information on how to link pay back mechanisms to employment contracts
	developing employer loan systems
	the reworking of tax relief on employer investment in training worth around £3bn per year
	issuing of best practice on internal and external employer-based employee development programmes
	encouraging all sectors to develop skill scoreboards
Encouraging trade unions to place training on the bargaining agenda	encouraging trade unions to bargain for workplace training committees, paid time-off for study
	increasing the union learning fund and bargaining for skills to increase the number of learning representatives
Business support policies	examining the impact of the national minimum wage on small firms and assess whether training interventions could increase labour productivity
	ensuring that that the SBS and the Business Link network develop an effective business support strategy which increases product development and innovation rates which in turns drives-up employer skill demand
	encouraging the rationalisation of chamber movement to deliver more effective private sector business support services which in turn drives-up employer skill demand
	ensuring that the SBS franchises and Business Link network market publicly funded training opportunities effectively
	ensuring that business advisers are fully conversant with workforce development strategies, policies and products
	examining the extent to which e:commerce drives up employer skill demand
	examining the extent to which e:commerce can reduce training costs
	creating a strong working relationship between the SBS and the Ufl so that the latter can deliver e:learning matertials required by employers after implementing business strategies designed by SBS Partnerships
	offering public subsidies to encourage employers to introduce the Business Excellence Model
	creating close links between regional cluster strategies and regional skills strategies

Figure 10.2 Options for statutory employer frameworks

Employability	Policy Measure	Description
	right to paid study leave	legislation giving every employee aged 18 and over the right to paid study leave including time-off for learning representatives
	workplace training committees	legislation to require every firm above a certain size to have a statutory training committee
	compulsory employer contributions to the national framework of individual learning accounts	legislation requiring all employers irrespective of sector and size to contribute x% of employers' national insurance contributions to the current national framework of individual learning accounts
Skills	Policy Measure	Description
training levies	national levy-grant system	legislation requiring every employer to pay a nationally set levy based on x% of employers' national insurance contributions with redistribution via a national, regional or local skills agency
	national remissible training levy system	legislation defining remissibility in terms of investment in training equivalent to x% of employers' national insurance contributions with the option of a link to, say, achievement of Investors in People
	exemption from the chosen system of financial contributions on evidence of involvement in one or more designated training activities	legislation requiring every employer above a certain size, say 10 employees, to demonstrate evidence of involvement in one or more of modern apprenticeships, the national framework of individual learning accounts, the University for Industry, Investors in People and employee development schemes, or contribute x% of employers' national insurance contributions under a levy-grant, remissible levy of compulsory individual learning account system
	targeted training tax on specific industrial sectors	legislation requiring every employer within specifically designated industrial sectors to be part of a levy-grant or remissible training levy based on x% of employers' national insurance contributions
Information and Compliance	Policy Measure	Description
disclosure of information	requirement to publish training information into company accounts	legislation to require every firm above a certain size, say more than 49 employees, to disclosure information on training in their company accounts including total financial spend, time-off for training and involvement in modern apprenticeships, the national framework of 'voluntary' individual learning accounts and the University for Industry

contract compliance	limiting government contracts to holders of IIP	legislation limiting government contracts to holders of Investors in People
	limiting access to European Funding to holders of IIP	legislation limiting access to European Funding to holders of Investors in People
Business support	*Policy Measure*	*Description*
	compulsory membership and subscriptions to sector or local employer bodies	legislation requiring compulsory membership of, and subscriptions to, sector or local employer bodies which funding used to provide SMEs with business development and innovation strategies which drive up employer skill demand

Figure 10.3 Training levy options	
Option 1	A Generalised UK Training Levy
Option 2	A Generalised Territorial/Regional Training Levy
Option 3A	A Generalised Sector Training Levy
Option 3B	A Generalised Sector Training Levy with In-Built Flexibilities
Options for flexible sector training levies	
Option 4A	An *Imposed Levy in Identified Sectors without In-Built Flexibilities*, where the Secretary of State would impose a levy in sectors identified as having a poor training performance, and decide on a sector by sector basis on the design features described above
Option 4B	An *Imposed Levy in Identified Sectors with In-Built Flexibilities* where each identified sector is empowered to decide on the levy design:
Option 5A	A *Statutory Regular Ballot for Sector Levies with In-Built Flexibilities*, where every sector would be balloted, say, every five years to introduce a training levy with each sector having discretion on design
Option 5B	A *Statutory One-Off Ballot for Sector Levies with In-Built Flexibilities*, where every sector would be balloted on a one-off basis to introduce a training levy
Option 5C	A *Statutory One-Off or Regular Ballot in Identified Sectors with In-Built Flexibilities*, where the Secretary of State would insist on a statutory ballot or regular ballot in identified sectors
Option 6A	*Encouragement of Voluntary Sector Training Levies without Statutory Underpinning* – the Government would encourage voluntary sector training levies which would not necessarily have a statutory underpinning
Option 6B	A *Sector Request for a Statutory Levy with In-Built Flexibilities*, where a sector would seek to build a voluntary agreement and request a statutory levy

References

The paper is largely derived from a series of research programmes and project reports undertaken by MC Consultancy for a range of clients

Campaign for Learning (2000) *The Manifesto for Family Learning* CfL, September

DfEE (November 2000) *Time Off for Study or Training: Preliminary Evaluation of the Implementation of the Employment Right* DfEE, Research Brief 221.

DfEE (2001) *Opportunity and skills in the knowledge-driven economy*

DTI (2000) *Parents and Work: Competitiveness and choice*

HM Treasury (2001) *Budget 2001: Investing for the Long Term: Building Opportunity and Prosperity for All*

National Skills Task Force (2000) *Skills for All: Proposals for a National Skills Agenda.* DfEE

11. Achieving quality jobs for all: new policy instruments
Nick Burkitt

There is no necessary contradiction between believing that any job is better than being unemployed, and thinking that being in a fulfilling and decently paid job is better than an insecure, low paid, dead-end one. Any government concerned with social justice, quality of life and long term prosperity cannot be content to see large numbers of its citizens trapped permanently in precarious, low paid, low skill jobs with no opportunity for advancement. There is evidence that up to a tenth of the British workforce spend their entire working lives in a cycle of disadvantage, moving between low paid jobs, often with spells of unemployment of inactivity in between (Meadows, 2000).

Getting people off state benefits should not be enough. The desire for a better work-life balance, better workplace relations, and more training and development opportunities cannot be confined to the better paid parts of the workforce.

This chapter looks at two particular ways in which the Government can make a commitment to both quality and quantity of work a reality, especially at the lower end of the labour market. The two sections each deal with a potential policy instrument, the first – the Working Age Agency – is to be created, and the second – an employment rights enforcement agency – is a proposal.

- The *Working Age Agency* will be formed in Autumn 2001 from a merger of the Employment Service and parts of the Benefits Agency. This new body, to be branded as 'Jobcentre Plus', will have the job of overseeing the development of welfare to work and 'New Deal II' over the next few years. It will also be the main point of contact between the state and everyone claiming in-work or out of work benefits who is not a child or a pensioner, as well as employers.

  One of the big questions is how far it could or should concern itself with people who have left benefits for work. There is growing discussion of the need for 'aftercare' to help people stay in work and even move on to higher paid positions with better prospects. This would mean significant extra resources, which implies a trade off with the goal of directing more help to the most disadvantaged people still outside paid work.

- A proactive *employment rights enforcement agency, or 'Fair Employment Commission'*. Enforcement of the government's 'minimum infrastructure of fairness and decency' based on individuals taking cases to Employment Tribunals has left out many people who should be protected by it. At the same time employers, especially small ones, need more help in meeting their obligations to their staff. This chapter discusses the case for a new organisation that could make legal entitlements like paid annual leave, sickness and maternity pay or rest breaks a reality for many people who have not been able to access their minimum rights through the current system.

More carrots *and* sticks for jobseekers and employers?

These two government bodies – one definite and one possible – raise some key questions about how the state influences what goes on in the labour market. Many of the preceding chapters have discussed different ways of influencing employers' and employees' behaviour, including both statutory and voluntary measures. Some policies are sold using the 'business case', as ways of encouraging firms or individuals to act in their own enlightened self interest- for example on Work-life Balance. Some are designed to achieve social ends that the labour market would not otherwise produce, such as the National Minimum Wage or maternity rights.

The political climate is not at present particularly conducive to significant extra regulation on the scale of the period of 1998 to 2000. In many areas, however, there is pressure for positive support and advice for businesses and individuals alongside existing compulsion or setting of minimum standards. This fits in with the government's rhetoric of greater 'rights and responsibilities' in many policy fields.

Both of the agencies discussed here will face the problem that they are offering their client groups both more help and the potential for more punitive measures than before. There is a danger that the threat of compulsion undermines the positive relationship. The Working Age Agency will offer more help with jobsearch and training, but it comes with the threat of benefit sanctions for non-co-operation. If this is handled wrongly, clients will become distrustful of the advice and guidance, even when it is genuinely in their best interests. Similarly, in its job of guaranteeing access to employment rights, the proposed enforcement agency will have to offer employers help in meeting their legal obligations. But this must be handled in such a way that business are not discouraged from approaching public bodies like the Small Business Service for fear of prosecution.

The legitimacy of strengthened compulsion on jobseekers or regulation of employers depends partly on the compensating offer of help by government to meet the new standards, but the precise nature of the link between them will have to be managed with great sensitivity.

1. Welfare to work

Building the Working Age Agency will be a major undertaking if it is to achieve the objectives set for it. Despite this, there has been relatively little public or political interest in its formation – perhaps because of the apparently administrative nature of the merger and the lack of a title for it until April 2001. It does however raise big questions about the future of welfare policy and the relationship between the state, individuals and employers. This chapter sets out the government's plans, and looks at what the agency could and should aim to do in the medium and longer term.

Existing objectives and plans for the Working Age Agency

In March 2000 the Prime Minster announced the creation of the Working Age Agency as 'the next stage of welfare reform, which will radically change the way the Government provides support for people of working age'. He said that it would 'have a new culture and will be firmly focused on helping people to become independent' (DSS, 2000). At the same time Social Security Secretary Alistair Darling described it as 'an essential part of our welfare strategy: changing the culture of the benefit system and moving from passive payment to active help for everyone of working age' (DSS, 2000). Giving evidence to the Commons Select Committee on Social Security, he enunciated the goals of the agency.

> There are two aims. One is to get people into work, and that is one of the criteria on which the organisation will be judged, just as our New Deals are going to be judged that way, through the present regime. The second is to make sure that we pay the right benefit to the right people. (Minutes of Evidence 3 July 2000)

The Public Service Agreement targets for 2001-4 under the heading of 'achieving employment opportunity for all' have been set out in Chapter 2. The objectives, which the Treasury, DfEE and DSS are jointly responsible for, are:

I   to increase the effective labour supply by moving as many additional unemployed people and inactive welfare recipients as possible into jobs and active competition for jobs

II   to counter poverty and social exclusion by helping welfare recipients facing the most severe disadvantages to compete effectively for jobs.

The Working Age Agency will be one of the main instruments for achieving both of these objectives. The Green Paper, 'Towards full employment in a modern society', announced plans to improve the New Deal programmes, and to 'extend more help and more choices to those who have traditionally been neglected: lone parents, people with disabilities and those suffering the greatest disadvantages in the labour market, as well as targeting extra resources on the communities that have been left behind' (DfEE, 2001). To help achieve this, it announced that the Agency was to be established in Autumn 2001, with a network of 50 pathfinder offices. Aside from the target of 70 per cent employment among lone parents by the end of the decade, there are no specific targets of the kind suggested in Chapter 2.

Responsibility for designing and developing the new agency is held jointly by the Secretaries of State for Education and Employment, and Social Security. A project team working from the Treasury and led by Richard Lapthorn, a former businessman, co-ordinated the early stages of the design process but in March 2001 Leigh Lewis, Chief Executive of the Employment Service, was named as head of the new agency.

Clearly, all three departments will retain a close interest in the objectives of the Agency and its day to day running, but it is still not clear precisely how the reporting structure will work. If one department is given overall charge, it is likely to affect the priority given to different objectives. A DfEE driven agency might be expected to be more 'work-focused' than one headed by the DSS. This also raises a wider question at the heart of government, about whether these two departments should be separate at all. The merging of employment with education is still a recent memory, but the logic of recent policy development might suggest a separate 'Department of Work', which might also take on some of the employment regulation functions currently carried out by the DTI. IPPR has been carrying out research on the possible remodelling of central government, but this book cannot attempt to deal with this.

The practicalities of a merger involving around 80,000 staff, two nationwide sets of offices and several incompatible and antiquated IT systems are likely to occupy the agency's attention for a long time. The details of medium and long term goals of the organisation will develop in time, in line with overall welfare policy and the requirements of delivering the existing benefits and job matching services. The Treasury design team said that what it hoped to achieve was not 'set in stone'[1] and would not be unchanging from day one of the agency's operation.

Within the overall goal of a desire to transform 'a passive benefit payment system into an active welfare state', there is some latitude for the role and day-to-day operation of the Agency to change over the coming years. It is also possible that there will be geographical variation in the way that the service operates, with some aspects of the service piloted in particular offices before becoming national, even after the network expands from the initial 50 pathfinder offices. This is how most welfare reform has been carried out under the Labour Government, with extensive trials, pilot schemes, and unprecedented resources put into evaluation and research.

The 'ONE' pilots have already been in operation since 1999, offering a unified service of exactly the kind planned for the Working Age Agency. These will provide the key lessons for the agency, although there will be the perennial problem that results achieved in pilots cannot always be recreated on a universal basis by large organisations.

The different labour markets and profiles of claimants across the country will also affect how far different possible goals are prioritised. A Jobcentre Plus office covering a town in the M4 corridor will clearly have more scope for considering issues like job progression than one in the Welsh valleys or Middlesborough, where the workload of sickness benefit payments and job seekers is much higher.

What should the Working Age Agency do?

There are a number of goals which the Agency might want to pursue, aside from its day-to-day activities of job matching (currently done by the Employment Service) and administering benefits (done by the Benefits Agency). These have the potential to conflict in their demands for time, staff and financial resources. The main ones are:

- reducing levels of inactivity, especially amongst lone parents, the over-50s and disabled people;

- 'retention'- keeping people in work rather than returning to benefits- and 'progression'- securing subsequent movement up the earnings and skill ladder for those who move into less well paid jobs;

- ensuring security for people who cannot work.

There is also likely to be tension between the needs and demands of employers trying to fill vacancies and the needs and desires of benefit claimants and jobseekers. All government employment services face a dilemma over the extent to which they are 'customer focused' (serving the needs of business), focus on policing benefits, or concentrate on helping the most disadvantaged (Thuy et al, 2001). The attempt to create a single work-focused service in one organisation will intensify this dilemma. The government has quite explicitly stated that it should have a greater focus on the needs of employers, but has also said it will direct more help to inactive groups and 'those suffering the greatest disadvantage in the labour market' (DfEE, 2001).

Chapter 2 argues that there is still some way to go before Britain can be considered to have full employment and that the government should be more ambitious in its employment targets. However, even if the employment rate reaches 80 per cent, its job will not be done. Ministers have increasingly accepted that it was not enough to judge the success of Welfare to Work simply in terms of the numbers who stop claiming benefits. Job retention – keeping a job and not just returning to benefits after a few weeks – and job progression – moving on to better paid, more satisfying work, with or without the same employer-have moved further up the agenda. The 'low pay/no pay cycle' has been seen to be alive and well, even in a tightening labour market and still need tackling.

This is linked to the question of how far programmes' objectives and evaluation should focus on enhancing long-term employability and how far they should focus on measures like job entry, completing work experience and gaining qualifications. These can be in tension with each other. Attempts to help the least job-ready can be undermined by failure to recognise 'distance travelled' towards employment. Failure to take time to find an appropriate match between job vacancies and job seekers can make jobs less sustainable. Although the 'jobs first' approach of the New Deals was strengthened in the early stages, the balance between job search and building 'human capital' can shift over time. It will also vary between client groups

In the 2001 Budget the Chancellor acknowledged the need to address 'progression in work', although it argued this is already being done through its lifelong learning and skills agendas, based on the Learning and Skills Council and instruments like Individual Learning Accounts and Learndirect (HM Treasury, 2001). Rather than proposing any major intervention in the short term, he announced an intention to run pilot projects over the next three years to learn about what works. There has been no official signal on whether or how the Working Age Agency, or its personal advisers, should be involved in supporting job progression once a client is placed in work. It would be possible for them to continue the relationship built up during job search programmes and help clients in jobs find careers advice, training courses or other job opportunities.

Arguably though, job retention is a more pressing issue than progression, and cannot be so easily separated from the goal of reducing unemployment and helping the most disadvantaged. If a significant number of people leaving benefits return to them within a few weeks or months, the welfare to work programme is not doing its job. Only 44 per cent of unemployed people entering a job stay in it for 12 months, compared to 59 per cent of all fresh starts. Unemployed people who enter work are three times more likely to subsequently (re)enter unemployment than those entering form another job (Boheim and Taylor, 2000). On the New Deals, 41 per cent of job starts have not been sustained. In other words only three fifths of jobs taken up last more than three months (DfEE, 2001b). There might be a role for Personal Advisers in offering counselling or moral support to help clients stay motivated in work and get through difficulties that could lead them to leave or be dismissed.

At the same time, it is clear that as the labour market tightens the amount of support needed by those still left outside it will tend to increase. Lone parents, disabled people and over-50s, although they are overlapping groups, face very different barriers to work, financial, psychological and practical. The smaller the number out of work, the more intense these barriers are likely to be. Extending compulsory participation in schemes to more groups of claimants will also tend to increase the level of resources needed. Bringing in people who are reluctant participants and are resistant to help on the New Deals has increased the time spent by Personal Advisers (Hasluck, 2000).

The needs of those in work and out of it will both make claims on government attention and resources in the next few years. It is likely that there will be a growing tension between the needs of a relatively small but heavily disadvantaged group still outside the world of paid work and the needs of those already in jobs but in constant danger of losing them and needing financial assistance to stay out of poverty. This raises a fundamental question about whether the focus of the Agency will be on employment or unemployment. A major element of this question is the nature of its relationship with the Learning and Skills Council, which replaced the Training and Enterprise Councils in April 2001, and the Further Education Funding Council. A significant practical factor affecting how well this partnership could work is whether the geographical boundaries of the different bodies' local operations coincide or not. This has not yet been resolved.

It is also important to remember the second part of the Government's slogan for welfare reform, 'Work for those who can, security for those who can't'. The clients using the agency will include people who are not in a position to take work, even if some might be able to in the future. They will include the most severely disabled, for whom paid work is not a possibility and who will always need a reasonable benefit income to sustain a good quality of life. There will also be people who have given up work to care for a sick or disabled dependent and simply want to claim their entitlement to benefits like Invalid Care Allowance. A 'work-focused' interview with a personal adviser on employment options would be inappropriate, and could undermine the relationship of trust between the agency and claimants.

The New Deal for Young people was from the outset compulsory for its client group. People aged 18-24 who had been on benefits for six months or more had to attend interviews with New Deal Personal Adviser, and then take up one of the four options, or face loss of benefits. Others such as the New Deals for Lone Parents and for Disabled people, began as voluntary schemes but from April 2001 lone parents have to attend in interviews with personal advisers or risk losing benefits. This extension of the principle of compulsion, which the Green Paper signalled will continue in the future, could well exacerbate fears that the government is only interested in forcing people off the benefit rolls, regardless of their needs. This is a danger that needs to be borne in mind both in the daily operation of the agency and in the political messages given out by ministers to the public.

Will it make a difference?

The formation of the Working Age Agency is being carried out in order to change the nature and quality of the service given to benefit claimants and to employers. The upheaval of such a large merger is only justified if the new organisation's output is greater than the sum of its parts. The New Deals have for the most part successfully overcome the cynicism of benefit claimants towards government schemes, but great care will have to be taken in widening the work focused service that this goodwill is not lost.

Personal advisers – the key to success

Almost all evaluations of the various elements of the New Deals and the 'ONE' pilots have found that the role of Personal Advisers is crucial (Hasluck, 2000). The government's plan is that 'eventually everyone of working age on benefit will have regular face-to face interviews with a Personal Adviser to discuss the possibility of work, with access to whatever help they need to help them obtain and keep in work' (DfEE, 2001). Depending on how 'regular' these interviews are, this will involve a significant increase in resources devoted to staff and training.

By the end of 2000, half a million people had joined the New Deal for young people, a third of a million had participated in the New Deal for Long-Term Unemployed, and 179,000 in the New Deal for Lone Parents (DfEE, 2001b). These numbers have been dealt with over a period of almost three years, but the stock of working age people on benefits is many times this number. There are just under one million JSA claimants, 2.9 million people on sickness and disability benefits and 900,000 lone parents on benefits. Even the New Deals have been coming up against problems with staff shortages. The demand for staff with advice, counselling, guidance and mentoring skills, which are not universally held by Employment Service personnel, has threatened to run ahead of the supply (Hasluck, 2000).

Evaluation evidence indicates that clients have been impressed by the helpfulness of NDPAs (New Deal Personal Advisers), and 'found the continuity and content of NDPA support well beyond their previous experience of the Employment Service or previous government schemes' (Hasluck, 2000). This has been true on national schemes, not just on pilots, where enthusiasm might be expected to be greater. Extending this further still to offer a service to all Working Age Agency clients without diluting the positive benefits will be a major challenge. This will involve significant retraining for ES and BA staff, and possibly new recruitment. Since the pay band which encompasses Personal Advisers in the Employment Service currently begins at around £14,000 per year, recruitment in parts of the country with tight labour markets will not be easy.

There are also difficult questions to be resolved over the role of Personal Advisers in meeting the needs of many different stakeholders. The new Agency is expected to be more employer focused than at present, but will also be attempting to deal with 'inactive' benefit claimants who will present many difficulties compared to existing JSA claimants. It will also be expected to build on and maintain links with private and voluntary sector providers of services, as the Employment Service has done with the New Deals and 'ONE'. One person cannot be expected to deal with all of these groups successfully, so the relationship between PAs and other staff or sources of information and services will be vital.

The focus on the most disadvantaged benefit claimants and inactive people will also emphasise the divergence in the needs of different client groups. Inevitably, advisers will have to specialise in clients with particular needs. Motivating a 19 year old who has never worked is clearly a very different job from helping someone adjust to a new career after becoming disabled in an accident.

The merger

Staff in the two organisations that will form the Working Age Agency have already been through a number of changes to their working practices and the service they provide in recent years. A great deal of attention will have to be paid to avoiding the 'implementation gap' of frustration among staff and clients due to lack of resources, heavy case loads, multiple targets and frequently changing government initiatives, issues that they have been concerned about in the past (Finn and Blackmore, 2001).

They will also bring different skills and experience, as well as distinct working cultures and different traditions of employment relations. One of the key differences, which could have a huge impact on the nature of the relationship between the new agency and its clients, is in the physical design of offices. Benefits Agency offices have security screens between staff and clients, while Jobcentres moved to open plan offices around ten years ago. The Public and Commercial Services Union, which represents both sets of staff, is opposed to forcing anyone to work without a screen, because of the possibility of violence from clients. This is one of the most contentious issues in the whole of the negotiations over transferring staff. Help with job search is clearly a very different kind of interaction from telling a desperate person that they cannot have the Giro cheque they were expecting. This again raises the question as to how truly integrated the Agency's service will be. Will there be separate parts of the office for advisers and counselling and for benefit transactions?

The merger also raises the issue of relationships with outside bodies. The prospect of further partnership with the private sector is viewed with unease by a number of existing BA and ES staff. A special conference called by the PCS union for its members in both organisation in January 2001 explicitly expressed its opposition to 'privatisation' either of 'welfare to work' programmes or internal functions, as 'morally wrong'. Privatisation is not being considered, but involvement of private and voluntary sector bodies in service delivery is well established in the New Deal programmes.

International lessons

The formation of the Working Age Agency in the UK is well in line with general international movements towards 'active welfare states' – aiming to improve employability rather than 'passive' policies of income support for unemployed people. It is also part of a general trend towards the bringing together of benefit and job search functions (OECD, 2001). A recent ILO report on Public Employment Services (Thuy *et al*, 2001) identified common trends towards:

- decentralising authority and responsibility to tap the energy of local staff and managers as well as adapt services more closely to needs;

- integrating services, with greater use of local one-stop shop; and

- competition in a market for service delivery

All of these elements have been included in UK Welfare to work programmes to some degree.

There has also been a widespread movement towards conditionality in welfare to work – the strengthening of responsibilities and obligations for benefit claimants, and weakening of the right to refuse job offers, but also offering more help than before. As discussed at the beginning of this chapter, it is widely felt that in order to demand more of benefit claimants, more has to be offered by the State in return.

A key lesson in terms of 'what works' from international evaluation of many schemes, is that job search assistance schemes have the most positive effects on the re-employment chances of participants. Training programmes and subsidies to employers are somewhat less effective and large scale public employment programmes have the least effects (Robinson, 2000). The question of whether institutional arrangements (like the WAA) are significant is still open (OECD, 2001).

There are also important lessons to be learned in relation to the process of forming a new agency or reforming the labour market. In New Zealand, for example, a Department of Work and Income was formed from a merger of government departments. It had a similar function of promoting 'welfare to work' as the new agency in the UK. It suffered from some major administrative problems in the early stages, with some benefits paid wrongly and not on time, causing a loss of public confidence. A Ministerial review by the new Government (Hunn, 2000) put this down partly to managers coming from an employment rather than social security background and taking an excessively 'gung-ho' approach to the reform. This report also commented that the new body was expected to take around four years to be working at full effectiveness. On this basis, the Working Age Agency in Britain will not be offering what ministers hope it will until 2005.

Australia is more unique, in that it is the only country to contract out the entire employment service, creating 'Centrelink' and the 'Job Network', but the process of reform there in the late 1990s also shows the importance of managing the process of setting up new institutions in this area. It is vital to manage the expectations of ministers and co-ordinating departments (in the UK: Treasury, DfEE, DSS) as to the rate of change possible, the levels of investment necessary and when dividends can be expected. It has also been found to be important to understand the cultural transition needed by staff, and to allow flexibility to take account of economic or policy changes over time.

This is important for the UK. A full Personal Adviser service for every single claimant will not be possible for some time, and politicians will have to avoid building up expectations the Working Age Agency cannot fulfil among the public and claimants. If both rights and responsibilities are to be increased, the services have to be built up in line with increased compulsion. Any moves to tackle retention issues and then progression will have to be rolled out carefully, as methods will have to be tried out, but also staff will have to learn new skills and acquire new knowledge.

Conclusion

The formation of the new Working Age Agency offers a great opportunity to help achieve genuine full employment, especially with the shifting of help towards inactive groups like lone parents, disabled people and over 50s. However, if it is to work in practice it will need very significant extra resources, especially in terms of staff training to meet the various demands on it from government, employers and benefit claimants. The process of setting it up and expanding its services will have to be handled with great care.

It will also create and intensify some tensions that policy makers will not be able to avoid and will have to balance. The key ones will be between:

- Helping inactive groups and the 'hardest to place' find work and attending to retention and progression for people who have already left benefits

- Offering personalised help and support and gaining clients' trust and policing benefit fraud or compliance with compulsory schemes

- Ensuring a 'work-focused' service and supporting people who cannot work

- Becoming more focused on employers' needs and more focused on the most disadvantaged.

Greater ambition for the new agency – welfare to *good quality* work

The first priority for government should be to get people in to work. Unemployment and economic inactivity are still unacceptably high in Britain. In general the effects of being out of work on people's mental and physical health are more damaging than being in a poor quality job. As Chapter 1 describes, full employment is also one of the best ways of raising working people's bargaining power, and therefore improving conditions of work. For all these reasons, and in the light of the likely practical difficulties of establishing it, the Working Age Agency needs to focus its efforts in the first few years on boosting its support to vulnerable and inactive groups.

However, right from the beginning the agency will need to be more ambitious than employment services have been in the past about getting people into good quality jobs and helping them progress to better ones. In the medium term the agency can get involved in providing clients services like careers advice and help with training after they have found work. Personal Advisers must be able to use their positive relationship with clients to help raise their ambitions and expectations of what they can achieve – and what they are entitled to – in work.

2. Access to employment rights for all: a new proactive enforcement agency

Earlier chapters have highlighted the benefits of full employment for the quality of jobs, especially for the people who are least in demand, by giving workers more bargaining power. They have also suggested various ways of improving aspects of the quality of work in areas such as work-life balance. The policy levers discussed include new or enhanced legal rights, as well as financial support and promotion of good practice by employers in one way or another. In many areas, the business case for better treatment of employees has been put forward, but it is clear that there are limits to it.

Although some employers may be unaware of the benefits of more sophisticated people management practices, some make a choice to base their business strategy on low cost, low value added production. Some calculate that the cost of better wages or better conditions for employees is greater than the value of savings on recruitment and retention or productivity (Brown *et al*, 2001). There are times where the state simply has to set minimum standards in the interests of social justice. There are also times when the economic interest of the country as a whole is not the same as that of individual businesses. All countries make choices about what level to set minimum standards in pay and conditions, which depend on their history and culture as well as economic factors. They can also make choices about how they enforce these standards.

The Labour government introduced a number of new employment rights between 1998 and 2000, but has paid less attention to the enforcement of them and of existing entitlements. The DTI Green paper on 'Work and Parents', for example, proposed a number of additions to existing maternity and parental rights at work, but did not address how these might be enforced, or acknowledge that not everyone gets their present statutory entitlements. This will be a major challenge for employment policy in the coming years

Who is missing out on their rights?

The extent of non-compliance with recent regulations is highly contested and is inherently difficult to measure. The available quantitative evidence on understanding and awareness of the various new employment rights is still limited and sketchy. The fieldwork for the Workplace Employee Relations Survey, the main representative study that could cover compliance by employers, took place between October 1997 and June 1998, a few months before the first of the new legislation took effect.

Even compliance with the National Minimum Wage is uncertain, despite being an apparently simple right that can be gauged in the various nationally representative surveys gathering pay data. The New Earnings Survey suggests 300,000 people earn below it (National Statistics, 2000), but this cannot be used as a measure of compliance. This is because exemptions or reduced rates apply for groups such as trainees and apprentices, and the survey data do not show who these people are. The Low Pay Commission's second report on the NMW asserted that 'the early indications are that the vast majority of businesses are meeting their obligations to pay the NMW, but not all workers entitled to it are receiving it'. A report for the DTI on the Working Time Regulations on the other hand, suggested that it had done little to change working practices, with employers in most cases using individual opt outs, derogations or collective agreements instead (Neathy and Arrowsmith,1999). In a survey by the CIPD, only two per cent of respondents working over 48 hours per week reported that their hours had been reduced to below 48 hours as a direct result of the regulations (CIPD, 2000).

There is evidence of significant non-compliance from the many advice agencies dealing with employees, such as the National Association of Citizens Advice Bureaux (NACAB), the Equal Opportunities Commission, Maternity Alliance and Low Pay Units. Inevitably it is only those who have a problem who ask for advice, so it is impossible to estimate the proportion of the workforce they represent. On the other hand there could be large numbers of people who never seek advice because they do not realise their rights have been infringed. The qualitative interviews described in Chapter 5 showed considerable lack of understanding of what are often complicated rights among working people, as well as lack of awareness of some of them. Participants in the groups also commonly described themselves or others settling for what they knew to be illegal discrimination or denial of rights through fear of losing their job, a desire not to 'rock the boat' or simply not knowing how to go about seeking redress.

Citizens' Advice Bureaux across Britain deal with 700,000 employment related cases per year and this figure is rising. The advisory and conciliation service ACAS receives over half a million enquiries on employment rights. NACAB has produced reports documenting the evidence these cases provide of weaknesses in the implementation of new and existing employment law (for example, Dunstan, 2000, 2001). It deals with large numbers of cases of people not receiving the National Minimum Wage, being denied their entitlement to four weeks paid leave or to maternity leave and pay, being forced or cajoled into 'opting out' of the 48-hour limit on weekly working time, and being discriminated against by their employer on account of their race, religion, sexuality, age or disability.

The people who make up the bulk of these cases are typically low paid and low skilled. They are rarely unionised (those who are would hopefully be able to seek redress with the help of their union). They are typically working in jobs such as care work, hairdressing, bar and hotel work, waiting, shop assistants and cleaning. These are exactly the less well paid service jobs that we can expect to see growth in over the coming years, as Adair Turner describes in Chapter 3.

It is also significant that many people complaining to the various advice services that they are missing out on one right also miss out on others. Many of those denied the minimum wage, for example, turn out not to be receiving holiday or sick pay (Low Pay Unit, 1999). This is not surprising, since the root cause is lack of bargaining power, which affects all aspects of reward from work.

Why do people miss out on their rights?

The main reason for introducing rights and minimum standards at work is that society wishes to protect people from the weakness of their position in the labour market. Although the relationship between an employer and an employee can be seen as a purely economic transaction, in practice societies have always recognised that it is too important to leave entirely to the market. The main reason for this is the imbalance of power. The labour market is often described as monopsonistic – there are relatively few buyers with a great deal of power. Most people have no choice but to offer themselves for paid work. This is of course far more the case for a worker with no formal qualifications living in Stockton-on-Tees than for an IT professional in Reading.

Rights and entitlements are put in place because the market outcomes that would occur in the absence of such rights would be socially unacceptable. By definition, people who need statutory protection will be in a weak bargaining position. This means that a system of enforcement based on individuals challenging their employer through a system of Employment Tribunals is likely to be of limited use.

Many of the people seeking help from advice agencies say they have been prevented from asserting their rights by the fear of losing their job. Some have been dismissed for asserting their employment rights. The only practical means of seeking redress for this is to bring a claim for unfair dismissal before an employment tribunal. The chances of reinstatement are minimal, and even those who succeed with such a claim are likely to be awarded a relatively small sum in compensation. Although the maximum compensatory award for unfair dismissal is £51,700, the great majority of awards are well below this upper limit. In 1999/00, when 3,168 cases of unfair dismissal were upheld by employment tribunals, the median award of compensation was just £2,515, and in 43.5 per cent of cases the award was less than £2,000 (Employment Tribunal Service, 2000).

Most people who might be entitled to take a case are well aware of this, and are put off by a daunting and adversarial tribunal system. They know that the process can be drawn out, extremely stressful and damaging to both sides. Evidence from Citizens' Advice Bureaux suggests that this is particularly the case for pregnant women and new parents who have been dismissed for pregnancy or denied maternity rights, since this is already a demanding and stressful time of their lives.

From the employers' side, there are a number of reasons why staff might miss out on their legal rights. These can range from straightforward lack of awareness of rights and who they cover, through misinterpretation of the law and inadvertent non-compliance due to inattention to people management issues in the face of other pressures on management time. Earlier chapters in this book have highlighted various forms of poor employment practice. Employers do not always use the people management techniques that research evidence and the most successful companies suggest are in their best interests. Many are unaware of how they could apply them to their own company. Many lack the time and resources either to find out about the law and best practice or to implement them-or at they least believe that they do.

This is especially likely to be the case for small employers, because they do not have the expertise in human resources issues or management time to spare. Some situations which call for an understanding of employment rights arise only rarely, especially in a small firm, so there is little incentive for employers to inform themselves of the details of provisions until it is too late. For example, businesses with fewer than ten employees are likely to have a pregnant employee only one year in ten. For those with 25 employees, the figure is one year in five (DTI, 2000)

However, there is also evidence of cases where poor practice or denial of entitlements is deliberate. There are undoubtedly unscrupulous employers who exploit their employees, denying maternity or sick pay, for example, with an implied or explicit threat of dismissal for those who object.

A new solution: the 'MOT for jobs' or Fair Employment Commission

Trade unions traditionally were the main way that employees redressed their lack of bargaining power. It is clear though that there is a large group of workers that unions are not reaching towards the lower end of the labour market. Thirty per cent of employees were union members at the end of the 1990s (National Statistics, 2000b), but in many areas of the private sector membership was rare. Less than one in ten employees in hotels and restaurants and other business services was a union member in 1998 (Cully et al, 1999). Even a dramatic increase in recruitment in these areas would leave a large proportion unprotected.

There already exists a model for a proactive enforcement agency that could fill the gap left by low rates of unionisation. The National Minimum Wage Enforcement Agency, operating within the Inland Revenue, should be built upon to create a new body that would help employees access all their rights at work.

There is growing momentum around the proposal for a new organisation that could act as a neutral auditor to ensure that employers are meeting their obligations to their workers. Acting at the level of the employer, rather than vulnerable individuals, it would resolve – and hopefully prevent – multiple breaches of statutory employment provisions. Like the existing Inland Revenue agency, it would investigate employers on the basis of individual, anonymous and third party complaints, as well as carrying out unannounced targeted inspections.

For it to work successfully, it must be seen to be neutral and also offer the prospect of positive help to employers to help them meet their statutory duties. As with the Minimum Wage at present, the Agency's Compliance Officers would have to enter the workplace as a representative of neither employer nor worker, simply aiming to check that the law is not being broken. They would then inform both sides if it was not and give clear guidance as to how to rectify the situation.

A useful analogy, which might help to sell the idea politically, is the 'MOT test' for cars. Drivers whose vehicles do not meet the legal standards are not immediately fined or prosecuted. They are told what the problem is and what they need to do to fix it. It is only if they fail to act on this that they are fined. A visit from the Compliance Officers, whether as a result of a complaint or random inspection, could be presented in this light, with enforcement measures only being used when evidence is found of the law being broken or rights being breached.

The early experience of the Inland Revenue in enforcing the Minimum Wage was that where complaints led to a detailed investigation beyond the initial contact with the telephone helpline, most employers complied after an initial approach from them.

Where they did not, the threat of enforcement action was frequently sufficient to achieve compliance. Only a few employers reached the point of penalty notices being served, and just a handful reached Employment Tribunals (Low Pay Commission, 2000).

Backing up enforcement with support

Because much non-compliance is unintentional, and employers are unaware of their obligations or believe they do not have the means to put them into practice, significant advice and practical support is likely to be needed. The Small Business Service (set up in April 2000) and the local Business Links offices already offer help, although their capacity in the area of human resources and people management might have to be expanded. There is also the idea, floated by the Chambers of Commerce, of 'locum personnel officers'. These could be state funded or subsidised and would join or work with employers to design new systems or practices and help get them underway. In many cases, half a day spent with an expert on the basics of Human Resources management would be enough to transform a small business' practices. This could be worth more than hundreds of leaflets and documents from the government offering guidance.

This could also have a wider benefit of spreading good employment practice into areas where it tends not to reach at present. The Work-Life Balance Campaign has found examples of employers who have simply not considered different ways of organising work and where small changes can have significant productivity benefits. This does not just mean small employers, but also those in low margin or low profitability sectors, where the scope for enlightened practice seems less.

There would need to be some kind of grace period for employers to implement changes to their practices where they were not meeting their obligations. In the case of the minimum wage, it is a relatively simple matter to pay someone extra, but where shift patterns and leave arrangements have to be rearranged to meet the Working Time Regulations, for example, an instant remedy is unlikely. With complicated regulations and staff on different terms and conditions, it could take time to establish what changes need to be made for whom, and then make them.

Where employers fail to respond to this action and continue to deny any of their workers their rights, the agency would have clear powers to impose financial penalties and if necessary to take workers' cases to employment tribunals or the courts.

There has been a long running debate in relation to the Equal Opportunities Commission (EOC), and Commission for Racial Equality (CRE), over the possibility and desirability of mixing compliance with advice and the spreading of best practice within one organisation (Hepple *et al*, 2000). Some believe that the two activities feed off each other and reinforce their impact, while employers have complained that charging a body with regulation and enforcement duties discourages them from applying to it for help.

The precise nature of the link between the new agency and the support to employers would be for government to decide after consultation with affected parties. It could be the case that Compliance Officers would be best used in signposting employers to the appropriate services rather than being seen to be involved in advice and guidance. What is clear, though, is that there would have to be extra resources put into advice services so that the promise of help could be kept. There would also have to be some form of co-ordination so that advice given by bodies like the Small Business Service or practices implemented by publicly funded consultants did not conflict with the work of the enforcement agency.

How would it fit in with the current system?

This new agency, perhaps under the name of the Fair Employment Commission, would build upon, but not replace, the activities of a number of public and statutory bodies. If it is to work effectively, it would also require significant extra public resources.

Setting up such a body would involve the transfer of existing functions, resources and staff from the Inland Revenue, the Department of Trade and Industry, the Department for Education and Employment, the Health & Safety Executive, local authorities and other governmental departments and agencies. It would also have considerable implications for other arms of government, such as the Advisory, Conciliation and Arbitration Service (ACAS) and the Employment Tribunal Service, as well as for the EOC, CRE and the Disability Rights Commission.

The reason for proposing this new instrument for government is not to supplant existing organisations and mechanisms. It is to reinforce the existing system and tackle some of its deficiencies. The equalities commissions already have a role which is not dissimilar in the area of equal opportunities. One of the key decisions for government in setting up this new body would be where the boundaries lay between them and how they might deal with workplaces where there is both discrimination and denial of other rights taking place. The new agency would deal with a specified list of rights, but not encroach on the equalities agenda. This list could include rights like those under the Working Time Regulations, the National Minimum Wage and Statutory Sickness Pay. The enforcement of some rights relating to maternity, parental and paternity leave and pay – and perhaps new ones arising from the Parents and Work Green Paper – are seen by some as equalities issues, but could be covered by the new agency. Giving entitlements to both sexes probably implies treating them as general employment rights rather than specifically women's issues.

The recent rise in the number of appeals to employment tribunals taking place has been seen as a cause for concern, especially by employers' groups. A new agency ought to help disputes be resolved earlier and reduce the number of complaints that go as far as a tribunal. By providing advice to employers and employees and enforcing compliance, it would remove the necessity for many individuals to take their cases to a tribunal in order to access their rights. On the other hand, it would still be necessary to resolve some disputes through tribunals, and some individuals might wish to continue down this route.

Conclusion

There is a clear gap in Labour's 'fairness at work' agenda around the issue of enforcing rights as well as introducing them. There need to be greater efforts to measure the extent of non-compliance, and to tackle it in a systematic way. This must involve recognition that people who need access to rights are by definition vulnerable, and that enforcement based on individuals taking an employer to a tribunal is never likely to be enough.

This gap could be filled with a new agency or 'Fair Employment Commission' which would:

- Proactively enforce a range of employment rights, acting on complaints (including anonymous and third party complaints) as well as using targeted random visits

- Act at the level of the employer, rather than the individual worker

- Investigate workplaces as a neutral auditor to check that the law and statute are being observed

- Offer help and support to employers to help them meet their obligations to employees

- Have powers to impose penalties and ensure compliance where employers still do not offer workers their rights and entitlements.

Endnote

1   *Working Age Agency – A Vision* Working Age Project Team presentation to IPPR seminar, December 2000

References

Boheim R and Taylor MP (2000) 'The Search for Success: Do the Unemployed find stable employment? *ISER Working Paper* 2000-5 Colchester, University of Essex

Brown D, Dickens R, Gregg P, Machin S and Manning A (2001) *Everything under a fiver: Recruitment and retention in lower paying labour markets* York, Joseph Rowntree Foundation

Chartered Institute of Personnel and Development (2000) *Working Time Regulations: have they made a difference?* CIPD

Cully M, Woodland S, O'Reilly A, Dix G (1999) *Britain at Work: as depicted by the 1998 Workplace Employee Relations Survey* London, Routledge

DfEE (2001) *Towards full employment in a modern society*

DfEE (2001b) *New Deal for Young People and Long-Term Unmemployed aged 25+: Statistics to December 2000* DfEE First Release February 2001

DSS (2000) Press release, March 16 2000

DTI (2000) *Work and Parents – Competitiveness and choice* A green paper

Dunstan R (2000) *Wish you were here: Evidence on the paid holiday provisions of the Working Time Regulations* NACAB

Dunstan R (2001) *Birth rights: A CAB evidence report on maternity and parental rights at work*

Employment Tribunal Service (2000) *Annual Report 1999-2000*

Finn D and Blackmore M (2001) 'Activation: the point of view of clients and "frontline" staff' in *Labour Market Policies and the Public Employment Service* OECD, Paris

Hasluck C (2000) *Early Lessons from the Evaluation of New Deal Programmes* Employment Service Research & Development Report, ESR49

Hepple B, Coussey M and Choudhury T (2000) E*quality: A New Framework. Report of the Independent Review of the Enforcement of UK Anti-Discrimination Legislation* Cambridge

Hunn D (2000) *Ministerial Review into the Department of Work and Income* New Zealand Government Website

Low Pay Commission (2000) *The National Minimum Wage: The Story so Far* Second Report of the Low Pay Commission, 2000 Cm4571

Low Pay Unit (1999) *The Low Paid and the Minimum Wage* Research Report to the Low Pay Commission

Meadows P (2000) 'Pensions and the Labour Market: How to help those on low lifetime incomes' in *New Economy* 7.4 Blackwell

National Statistics (2000) *The New Earnings Survey 2000* First Release

National Statistics (2000b) *Labour Market Trends* July 2000

Neathy F and Arrowsmith J (1999) *The Early Implementation of the Working Time Regulations – An Interim Report for the DTI*

Robinson P (2000) 'Active Labour-Market Policies: a Case of Evidence-based Policy-Making?' in *Oxford Review of Economic Policy* 16.1 Oxford University PressSocial Security Committee, (2000) Minutes of Evidence, 3 July 2000

Thuy P, Hansen E and Price D (2001) *The public employment service in a changing labour market* International Labour Office, Geneva